a healthier home

Inspiring | Educating | Creating | Entertaining

Brimming with creative inspiration, how-to projects, and useful information to enrich your everyday life, Quarto.com is a favorite destination for those pursuing their interests and passions.

First Published in 2022 by Fair Winds Press, an imprint of The Quarto Group,
100 Cummings Center, Suite 265-D, Beverly, MA 01915, USA.
T (978) 282-9590 F (978) 283-2742 Quarto.com

Fair Winds Press titles are also available at discount for retail, wholesale, promotional, and bulk purchase. For details, contact the Special Sales Manager by email at specialsales@quarto.com or by mail at The Quarto Group, Attn: Special Sales Manager, 100 Cummings Center, Suite 265-D, Beverly, MA 01915, USA.

26 25 24 23 22   2 3 4 5

ISBN: 978-0-7603-7760-4

Digital edition published in 2023
eISBN: 978-0-7603-7761-1

Library of Congress Cataloging-in-Publication Data

Names: Holman, Shawna, author.
Title: A healthier home : the room by room guide to make any space a little less toxic / Shawna Holman.
Description: Beverly, MA : Fair Winds Press, 2022. | Includes index. | Summary: "In A Healthier Home, Shawna Holman, founder of A Little Less Toxic, provides an inspirational yet achievable approach for making the home a safer space"-- Provided by publisher.
Identifiers: LCCN 2022026252 | ISBN 9780760377604 (hardcover) | ISBN 9780760377611 (ebook)
Subjects: LCSH: Housing and health. | Sanitation, Household. | Orderliness.
Classification: LCC RA770 .H63 2022 | DDC 613/.5--dc23/eng/20220715
LC record available at https://lccn.loc.gov/2022026252

Design and Page Layout: Tanya Jacobson, jcbsn.co
Front cover: Shutterstock; Back cover: Matthew Bilbault
Photography: Matthew Bilbault

Printed in China

The information in this book is for educational purposes only. It is not intended to replace the advice of a physician or medical practitioner. Please see your health-care provider before beginning any new health program.

a healthier home

The Room-by-Room Guide
to Make Any Space
A LITTLE LESS TOXIC®

Shawna Holman

FAIR WINDS

Contents

Introduction

Welcome! I'm so glad you're here. Kick your shoes off and come on in. I hope these pages feel like a good friend's home—a place you can rest knowing you are accepted as well as a place where you will be challenged to make some changes for a better life along the way. I also hope that rather than being read start to finish, this book should feel like a place you can come and visit whenever you like. This book was written for you right where you are on your journey toward a healthier home and life. From those of you who have never considered any of these ideas before, to those who are "A Little Less Toxic" pros, all are welcome here, and I know you'll find help and encouragement within these pages. I wrote these words so they might help as you let go of whatever isn't serving you and invite more goodness into your life and home.

This is not a book I expect anyone to read and implement *every part of*, and definitely not all at once.

I certainly haven't approached a less toxic life that way. For me, it started after years of chronic migraines or sinus infections. The pharmaceutical interventions that came along with them led to a common infection almost taking my life. At that point, I became desperate for change and began to take matters into my own hands. I took a closer look at what I was inviting into my home and onto and into my body and began to implement simple lifestyle changes. I made one or two swaps at a time and as budgets allowed.

And, as it turned out, the simple swaps had a tremendously positive effect on my health and life. In a short time (think days, not months!), I was pain-free for the first time in years. It rocked my world and gave me so much hope, not just for myself, but for everyone I knew and loved who had mystery health issues, too. I made my first swap in 2013 and have continued on the path ever since.

My home is still far from perfect. I don't believe we will ever live in a perfectly nontoxic home—definitely not in this modern world. I am confident, however, that making mindful choices about what we bring into our homes will make positive changes on our health and quality of life. I've also witnessed other lives be transformed because of these seemingly small changes time and time again. I want more health, freedom, hope, and joy for everyone. I know that what we have and use in our homes matters, and I want to share this resource with anyone who is ready to make one small change and just keep going.

If this book makes you feel over-whelmed, stick it in a closet for a while. If it continues to worry you, get it out of your hands and home, immediately. Stress is more toxic than just about anything I talk about here. This is not a book to add any kind of stress or worry to your life. This is a tool for you to use at your convenience and as it makes sense for you. And, I hope this will be a well-loved resource for you to return to time and again as you make healthy swaps in your home. These pages will be here to help you make informed decisions any time you want to replace something you're running low on or that wears out or when you make updates or home projects or renovations.

Join me as we take one day, one meal, one product at a time, and make our homes and lives A Little Less Toxic. Always remember: Do what you can, with what you're able, and as it makes sense for you.

love,
Shawna

Quick Start Guide

My top 3 tips to make your home healthier instantly:

1   Open windows and/or doors daily for 10 to 20 minutes. Twice a day is best. Let trapped and polluted air out and fresh air cycle in. Even in cities with poorer air quality, doing so can improve indoor air.

2   Leave shoes off indoors. Shoes can bring a lot of unwanted bacteria and toxic materials into the home via the surfaces.

3   Make swaps along the way that are sustainable and reasonable for your circumstances and budget. Just keep going. Follow the **ALLT**, (A Little Less Toxic), approach to make this a manageable lifelong practice:

(A) **Assess:** Take inventory and consider which items are actually used. Keep only things you really need. Note: Once you get better at this process, I can almost promise this list will become even shorter over time.

(L) **Let go:** If it's expired or unnecessary and contributing to clutter and/or toxic burden, find it a new home. That may very well be the garbage.

(L) **Level up:** As an item runs low or needs to be replaced, look for an alternative with healthier ingredients. Do not wait until you're at empty, otherwise you'll most likely grab the same old thing or something with compelling marketing on the label.

(T) **Transform over time:** As soon as you get rid of one item or replace it with something healthier, your space is immediately less toxic! Over time, this will multiply and compound—watch how quickly small things add up.

Oh, and read ingredients, not marketing claims. It's what's inside that counts. Sites and apps like EWG (Environmental Working Group) and Think Dirty can be helpful for scanning items or looking into individual ingredients to help you become a more informed consumer.

Feel free to visit my site, alittlelesstoxic.com, for up-to-date product recommendations, discounts, recipes, and a resource page full of free downloads.

What *is* Toxic?

Our bodies are designed to be able to filter toxins through the colon, kidneys, liver, lungs, lymph, skin, and spleen. These important players capture, filter, and remove toxins from the body. And I have to say they are magnificent at doing this, especially in a balanced body and a healthy environment. However, it is becoming ever more difficult to maintain that balance as these detox organs are being asked to take on loads like never before. The demand on our bodies is increasing. The capabilities of our detox systems are often compromised because of the volume of input. Our capacity to store toxins and toxicants as our bodies work to excrete them can vary from one person to the next. Factors that contribute to our toxic load capacity include age, ethnicity, gender, and genetics. Our ability to process and excrete these invaders is partly determined by those factors and also by external influences, including cumulative exposure, illness, stress, and trauma.

When we take on more toxins than we can effectively eliminate, the load becomes a burden. The body will attempt to balance by becoming inflamed as defensive and protective measures. Unchecked, this inflammation can lead to other issues.

Where are all these toxins coming from? Some toxicants are found in manufactured and extracted substances. These can include byproducts, chemicals, cleaning agents, emissions, pesticides, and more. The source can also be anything that produces a toxic effect. These potentially harmful substances are presently part of everyone's existence. Newborn umbilical cord blood has been reported to contain upwards of two hundred chemicals.

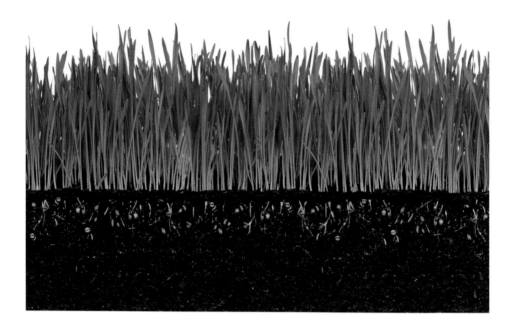

Toxins are also naturally occurring. They are produced by living organisms like bacteria, fungi, insects, mold, parasites, and plants. These substances have always existed and will always be part of nature. This means, too, they are part of everyone's existence, even before birth.

Before your head starts spinning, wait! Stress is not the goal here. In fact, stress only adds to the load. This whole book is about small steps. We'll take it one item, one meal, and one day at a time. Small changes add up quickly and can make a huge positive impact. My goal is to slow the flow of that which my body has to contend with. I aim to make informed choices to help me feel well, live well, and serve well. This has helped me live with less discomfort and pain, more energy, more clarity, and generally just . . . better!

I do not like to focus on what is wrong, but rather on what is good and what we can do to make things better. Yet, this chapter is very important and can't be left out. The following pages provide information that will be useful to understand what may be contributing to your toxic burden. Information is powerful and can help us become more educated and informed consumers. It will provide a reference to return to as you read through other topics or chapters and as you go about your life, making it A Little Less Toxic.

On Toxins and Terminology

What we use on, in, and around our bodies is important. Reducing exposures and lowering our cumulative load is the name of the game after all (and probably why you're reading this book!). How many products do you apply to your skin in one day? What ingredients are contributing to the toxic load instead of to healing? How many items in your home or office have fragrance? Parabens? Phthalates? BPA? PFOAs? Flame retardants?

There are numerous ways toxins get into our system:

- Absorption, through the skin or eyes
- Inhalation, through the mouth or nose
- Ingestion, entering through the mouth via food, drink, supplements, medications, or other
- Injection, entering the bloodstream via puncture, cut, or abrasion

Additionally, we're not the only ones living in our homes. A microbiome is a community of microscopic organisms. Most of us have heard of the human microbiome, but there are countless microscopic organisms on the surfaces in our homes as well as on and in our bodies. These organisms serve great purposes, and keeping them protected and balanced is for our good. The balance of the ecosystems of these organisms we cannot see is critically important for our health. Overuse of

sanitizers disrupts this balance. The exposure to and use of toxins, while clearly having the ability to negatively affect us, can have consequences for the microscopic organisms we depend on for health and survival as well. I can go on and on about the microbiome (and often do!), but my point for this chapter is this: Consider the microbes when thinking of your health and the health of your home.

Important Terms

Byproduct: Something produced in the making of something else.

Carcinogen: Any substance or agent that tends to produce a cancer.

Endocrine disruptor: A natural or synthetic chemical that mimics or blocks the action of a natural hormone and that may disrupt the body's endocrine system.

Environmental toxin: A small amount of a poisonous substance found in air, food, water, etc.

Flavor: Additional flavor compounds, contained in the vast majority of processed foods, used in food products to produce smells and tastes and manipulate and enhance the taste of the end product. Flavor companies own the proprietary formulas of these concoctions, which may include upwards of dozens to more than one hundred individual ingredients, all under the umbrella of "flavor"—whether artificial, natural, organic, or otherwise, and that may include ingredients such as BHA, BHT, diacetyl, and polysorbate 80. These "flavors" are trade secrets and protected, meaning finding out what the term "flavor" actually comprises in any given product is virtually impossible.

- **Artificial flavors:** Synthetic ingredients made in a lab designed to mimic the taste of natural ingredients or manipulate the taste of the end product. According to the U.S. Food and Drug Administration, artificial flavor is: "Any substance, the function of which is to impart flavor, which is not derived from a spice, fruit or fruit juice, vegetable or vegetable juice, edible yeast, herb, bark, bud, root, leaf or similar plant material, meat, fish, poultry, eggs, dairy products, or fermentation products thereof."

These artificial flavors are often less expensive to produce and more stable from a chemical standpoint, which means they are advantageous to the manufacturer. The term is used to indicate proprietary chemicals owned by the flavor makers that create them. Their individual ingredients need not be fully disclosed to protect proprietary information as long as the ingredients used have been deemed GRAS (generally regarded as safe) by the FDA.

- **Natural flavors:** Natural flavors are derived from substances found in nature, which may include animal parts, petroleum, wood pulp, and other materials we'd generally not choose to put in our food. They may also contain emulsifiers, preservatives, solvents, stabilizers, and other incidentals. Sometimes natural flavors may also be less sneaky ingredients like vanillin or maple extract. Look for non-GMO natural flavors from companies you trust and get comfortable asking companies questions.

- **Organic natural flavors:** Natural flavors that meet organic guidelines mean at least 95 percent of the ingredients must be organic, with no synthetic solvents, carriers, or artificial preservatives. Organic natural flavors cannot contain additives such as benzoic acid, BHA, BHT, medium chain triglycerides, mono- and diglycerides, polyglycerol esters of fatty acids, polysorbate 80, propylene glycol, or triacetin.

Fragrance: This is an umbrella term that covers combinations of chemicals that produce scent in a product. Those chemicals may be natural and/or synthetic ingredients and may contain upwards of hundreds to thousands of individual ingredients that need not be disclosed under protection of propri- etary recipes. The U.S. Department of Health and Human Services claims there are more than five thousand different fragrance chemicals and they may be used in countless combinations. And although the ingredients receive a GRAS label, many may be problematic and potentially contribute to health issues. Fragrance is ubiquitous, as it can be found in many common items throughout the home, including air

fresheners, body cleansers, candles, clothing, cosmetics, detergents, feminine hygiene products, household cleaning products, personal care products, shaving creams, soaps, toys, trash bags, and more. Many fragrances contain ingredients of concern, includ- ing carcinogens, endocrine disruptors, neurotoxicants, phthalates, and volatile organic compounds (VOCs).

Note: Fragrance is the number-one cause of contact dermatitis according to the American Academy of Dermatology.

Mutagen: An agent, such as a chemical or various radiations, that tends to increase the frequency or extent of mutation.

Off-gas: To give off a harmful gas.

Reproductive toxin: Any hazardous chemical or material that adversely affects reproductive organs.

Common Toxins Found in the Home

Many of these common toxins are listed in various places throughout this book.

Benzene: The U.S. Environmental Protection Agency (EPA) has classified benzene as a Group A, known human carcinogen. It is widely used in the United States, ranking in the top twenty chemicals for production volume, and it is used in many other countries. It is commonly used in the production of other chemicals, including detergents, drugs, dyes, lubricants, pesticides, plastics, and rubbers. Over the last couple of years, benzene has been making major news as it continues to be detected in very popular brands of personal care products, including deodorant and sunscreen, leading to large-scale recalls of such products.

Bisphenol A (BPA): The EPA states that BPA is found to be a developmental, reproductive, and systemic toxicant in animal studies and is weakly estrogenic. It is produced in mass quantities, primarily for use in plastics, including for food containers and the inner linings of canned goods, eyewear, feminine hygiene products, personal care products, receipt paper, sports equipment, toys, and more. Some research indicates BPA can leach from containers to contaminate food, especially when exposed to heat.

Bisphenol F (BPF) and **Bisphenol S (BPS):** Plastic items with a BPA-free claim, most likely, have switched to BPF or BPS following concerns and consumer demands regarding BPA. Research suggests these alternatives may have similar implications and are not much, if any, better.

Chloramine: This combination of chlorine and ammonia is typically used as a secondary disinfectant in municipal drinking water. It can provide longer-lasting disinfection as the water travels through pipes to get to our homes, yet it may have negative health effects similar to chlorine.

Chlorine: One of the most commonly manufactured chemicals in the United States, chlorine is found in virtually all homes, not just those with pools. Chlorine is the main ingredient in bleach and, thus, is found in many common household cleaners and disinfectants. It is also used in municipal tap water to kill bacteria. Chlorine is a potent irritant to the eyes, lungs, respiratory tract, and skin.

According to the Association of Occupational and Environmental Clinics, chlorine is an asthmagen, meaning it can contribute to and exacerbate respiratory issues and has been connected to some respiratory cancers.

Chlorine may pose a greater risk when the water is heated, as vapors are created that we then breathe in. Bleach also does not play well with others and, when used in combination with other common household cleaners, including even vinegar or alcohol, it can create noxious fumes, chloramine gas, chloroform gas, and other toxic and dangerous results. Contrary to popular belief, bleach is not even a great choice for killing mold as it can actually contribute to mold growth instead (especially in porous materials). Although chlorine bleach may kill and lighten surface mold stains, it can add to the moisture beneath the surface and exacerbate any hidden mold.

Formaldehyde: Recognized as a human carcinogen, this chemical preservative is commonly used in building materials, clothing, manufactured wood furniture, and many household products like carpeting, caulks, cosmetics, drapery, glues, paints, and upholstery. Short-term exposure effects have been well studied and can include harm to skin, respiratory passageways, and eyes. Less is known about long-term health issues at this time, though there are studies showing links to more severe health outcomes, including some cancers.

Heavy metals (such as aluminum, arsenic, cadmium, chromium, lead, mercury, and others): These naturally occurring metallic elements weigh at least five times more than water.

They are used in domestic, industrial, medical, technological, and other applications, which all have contributed to widespread distribution of these elements. This has not only led to the increased prevalence of heavy metals in the home and elsewhere, but has also raised concerns over potential risk to human health. Heavy metals are commonly found throughout the home in bowls, cups and plates, cookware, cosmetics, furniture, mattresses, paint, rugs, and water.

Herbicides: This term is used to describe chemicals that control undesired vegetation. Usually, herbicides are a synthetic mimic of plant hormones made up of chemicals that may pose health risks and environmental concerns.

Parabens: Common parabens include butylparaben, ethylparaben, methylparaben, and propylparaben. All are man-made chemicals used as a preservative. They are commonly found in cosmetics and personal care items such as cleansers, moisturizers, shampoos, and sunscreens, as well as other household items, including some pharmaceuticals, foods, and beverages. Although studies are lacking, a main concern is the potential for parabens to act like estrogen in the body and disrupt hormones, making them potential endocrine disruptors. Some reports suggest potential links to fertility issues, reproductive health concerns, and increased risk of some cancers.

Per- and polyfluoroalkyl substances (PFAS): This group of manufactured chemicals has been in use since the 1940s and is gaining a reputation as "forever chemicals" because they break down very slowly and can accumulate in animals, people, water, and the environment over time. These chemicals can be commonly found in water, soil, and in many places throughout our homes, including dust, food, furniture, and household items. Current peer-reviewed scientific studies have shown that exposure to certain levels of PFAS may lead to reproductive effects, developmental effects or delays in children, decreased immune response to infections, hormone interference, and increased risk of some cancers, including kidney, prostate, and testicular cancers.

Perfluorinated chemicals (PFCs; such as Teflon): This large group of chemicals, whose main uses are to make materials resistant to grease, stains, or water, and to make items nonstick, is commonly found in bakeware, cookware, food containers, and some fabrics, including for auto upholstery, carpets, clothes, furniture, and mattresses and bedding. Widespread use has led to increased human exposure and concerns about negative health effects. Some concerns include adverse birth outcomes and reproductive issues, growth and development issues, and liver problems.

Pesticides: Any substance used to control, kill, or repel animals, insects, or plants considered a pest; pesticides can be natural or synthetic ingredients. Health concerns vary based on the ingredients and their use.

Petrochemicals: Chemical products derived from petroleum, a crude oil; commonly found throughout the home in items such as appliances and electronics, plastics, preservatives in food and food packaging, synthetic fibers in carpets, upholstery, and other textiles, synthetic rubber, such as the soles of sneakers, and personal care products and cosmetics (and not just *petroleum* jelly).

Phenol: These chemical compounds are found in small doses in many common items throughout the home. (This can include items containing BPA, parabens, and triclosan.) Phenol may be found in some personal care products, plastics, and wood products that contain adhesives. Some studies in journals such as *Environment International* and *Environmental Research* have identified phenols in the urine of children and in dust samples in the homes of these children.

Phthalates: These are chemical compounds commonly used in plastics to make them more flexible and durable. Phthalates are commonly detected in household items such as carpets, food packaging, plastic containers, raincoats, toys, and vinyl flooring. They are also commonly used to help fragrance bind to a product (and fragrance is ubiquitous in the home, including in air fresheners or home scents, candles, cleaning supplies, clothing, hygiene products, personal care items, toys, and more). These compounds have been established as endocrine disruptors, and in animal studies have shown reproductive system effects.

Polybrominated diphenyl ethers (PBDEs): These are industrial flame-retardant chemicals used in carpeting, consumer electronics, furniture, mattresses, and more. The EPA regards these as persistent, bioaccumulative, and toxic to both humans and the environment. They have been linked to health issues including delayed brain development, thyroid problems, and tumors.

Polyurethane: This is a polymer created post-WWII as a rubber replacement that has various types and functions. It can be found in coatings on wood floors and furniture, in furniture cushioning and most modern mattresses, shoe soles, sporting equipment, car seat cushioning, and more. Because it is highly flammable, it is almost always heavily treated with flame retardants like PBDEs (see previous).

Radon: An inert, colorless, odorless gas, radon is naturally occurring and not usually an issue outdoors. However, radon may become trapped and accumulate indoors. It is found in homes as it can seep through cracks or openings in the foundation. Testing

kits can be found at local hardware stores and they are inexpensive. There are professional teams that can test for radon and offer mitigation and repair steps as well. Radon is the second leading cause of lung cancer, according to the EPA.

Retinyl palmitate a.k.a. retinoic acid or vitamin A: Vitamin A is great to get from food. The synthetic version is added to many items found around the home, especially skincare products. In certain amounts, it may not be a problem. Studies indicate many people exceed daily safe amounts from food and supplements alone. As vitamin A is added to more and more skincare and cosmetic items, especially those marketed as "anti-aging," the risk of exceeding safe use increases. Excess levels have been linked to bone problems including osteoporosis and skeletal birth defects.

Sodium laureth sulfate, SLS: Though not a huge concern, SLS can cause irritation. It and other variations including SLES are used to keep oil and water ingredients from separating, to create foam, and for other purposes. There are several other surfactants that work well with less irritation potential, such as decyl or lauryl glucoside, when a surfactant may be needed. As far as foaming bubbles in products, they're usually not needed to be effective. Most of that idea came from marketing tactics because research found that people like bubbles and think things are cleaner when suds are present.

Triclosan: This is an ingredient added to many consumer products to reduce or prevent bacterial growth and contamination. Its use is so ubiquitous it is estimated upwards of 75 percent of the population is exposed to it regularly. Triclosan is commonly found in body washes and other personal care products, cleaning products, cosmetics, soaps, shampoos and conditioners, toothpastes, some clothing, and more. Excessive use can contribute to the growth of antibiotic-resistant bacteria. Some other potential health implications include autoimmune diseases, liver function impairment, and thyroid impairment or disease.

Volatile organic compounds (VOCs): These widely used chemicals can both vaporize into air and dissolve in water. They are commonly found in adhesives, air fresheners, building materials, carpet, caulk, composite wood, cosmetic products, furniture, paints and varnish, soaps, and vinyl flooring, many times contained under the umbrella term "fragrance." VOCs off-gas from products and materials and contribute to indoor air pollution. Studies in journals such as *International Journal of Environmental Research and Public Health*, *Reviews on Environmental Health*, and *Environmental Research* indicate links to pulmonary health effects and potential links to many health issues including several cancers.

Certifications

Most products come with claims and many boast certifications, especially those that are marketing toward consumers who want healthier materials, but many of those claims turn out to be hollow and misleading. Some do have value, though, and can help those who desire healthier products navigate purchases with more confidence. Here, I include some current certifications that I believe have value and describe what they mean.

eco-INSTITUT®

This German-based organization provides independent testing, analysis, and certification programs for manufacturers across a wide range of products, including bedding and mattresses, building materials, consumer goods, floor coverings, and furniture. Its certificate is awarded only to products that meet the strictest requirements for low emissions and pollutants.

GOLS® (Global Organic Latex Standard)

This nonprofit, international, third-party certification ensures latex is made of more than 95 percent certified organic raw material based on weight. GOLS certification also focuses on aspects such as factory workers' overall safety and health, and the environment in the manufacturing process. It examines emissions, filler percentages, polymer, and any substances deemed harmful. Common items include bedding products and mattresses, bands, condoms, gloves, rubber toys, shoe soles, and any other product made from organically grown natural rubber latex.

GOTS® (Global Organic Textile Standard)

GOTS is the worldwide leading textile processing standard for organic fibers, including ecological and social criteria, backed up by independent certification of the entire textile supply chain. GOTS-certified products may include clothes, fabrics, fiber products, home textiles, mattresses, personal hygiene products, and yarns as well as food contact textiles and more. GOTS-certified products must use organic fibers, meet specific ecological and social criteria, meet all of this at every stage of processing, and receive third-party certification.

MADE SAFE®

MADE SAFE® is a program of Nontoxic Certified, a 501(c)(3) non-profit organization. It is America's first comprehensive human health and ecosystem-focused certification for nontoxic products across store aisles—from baby to personal care to household and beyond. It screens ingredients for known behavioral toxins, carcinogens, endocrine disruptors, developmental toxins, heavy metals, neurotoxins, reproductive toxins, high-risk pesticides, VOCs, and more.

OEKO-TEX®

This certification comes from a conglomerate of independent institutes in Europe and Japan that continuously develop test methods and limit values for the textile and leather industries. It is a set of third-party certifications verifying that a product is tested throughout the manufacturing process for chemicals that are potentially harmful to humans and our larger ecosystems.

the Living Room
(*and* Other Shared Spaces)

The living room is the place where you step into most homes. In this book, I use the living room in a similar way. Over the following pages, I address some things that are unique to the living room. However, many of the topics I cover apply to other rooms in the house as well, from air quality to EMF exposure.

Because the topics are wide ranging—I cover everything from the air to paint, furniture, and floors—keep in mind that the goal is always to do what you can, with what you're able, and as it makes sense for you. There is no need to stress about not doing more. In fact, if you ever want to come back to what I consider the essentials, here is a simple list of achievable changes to improve your living room (and whole home!):

Avoid items with "fragrance"

Change HVAC filters on time

Check for water damage and mold

Dust regularly

Get ducts cleaned regularly (at least every couple of years)

Invest in a quality air filter and water filter

No shoes inside

Open windows

Shut off Wi-Fi at night

Use fewer toxic cleaning supplies

Vacuum regularly, ideally with a HEPA-filter vacuum

Indoor Air Quality

The U.S. Environmental Protection Agency estimates that 60 percent of homes are hazardous to their occupants' health, with indoor air being up to one hundred times more polluted than outdoor air. In fact, indoor air pollution is ranked among the top five environmental risks to public health. Most people spend upwards of 90 percent of their lives indoors, so this is not an issue to ignore. Fortunately, there is plenty you can do to improve your indoor air quality immediately and for the long term. Many steps you can take require minimal effort—and are free or very low cost. First, let's take a look at what causes poor indoor air quality and why it is so much worse that the air outside.

Why is indoor air so polluted? All homes are built to keep the inhabitants sheltered and protected from outside elements. They are designed to keep it cooler inside when it's hot out and trap heat in when it's cool out. This means that air is kept inside recirculating along with whatever has been added to the air through the materials, products, and residents living in the home. Modern homes are even built with specialized materials to be "energy efficient." This means they are extra good at keeping the desired temperature in (and the air contaminants, too).

The problem is, we have been polluting our indoor air with VOCs, including formaldehyde and gases from paint, varnishes, and adhesives from carpet, flooring, and rugs, building materials, caulk, composite wood, flooring, furniture, and more. Cleaning products, as well as toiletries and cosmetics, add their own chemicals to the mix. Air fresheners, scented candles, plug-ins, etc., pile it on. Then, there's dander, dust, dust mites, mold, and fumes and gases from cooking. Last but not least, different homes pick up varying levels of pollution from outside, including allergens, exhaust, smog, smoke, etc.

How to Improve Indoor Air Quality

In this section, you can probably find some things you can do right now to have an immediate and positive effect, and others you may choose to shift over time. Yet, each small change can add up to make an improvement. Some changes may take longer to deliver results and require more energy or financial investment to implement. Do what you can today and add more as you're able along the way, knowing that the small things are truly making a tremendous difference.

Avoid "fragrance": Skip the air fresheners, scented candles, and plug-ins with fragrance as an ingredient. They're full of endocrine-disrupting phthalates and VOCs. Choose items with less-toxic ingredients, diffuse essential oils, or make simmer pots with fresh fruits, herbs, and spices (for more on this, see page 41).

Check for water damage a.k.a. *mold*: Mold is a big contributor to poor indoor air quality as well as many health issues. Most people think mold is visible and only toxic if it is and if it's black. That's not true. Where there is water damage, there is mold. The spores of that mold contain mycotoxins, which can wreak havoc on health. Replace water-damaged wood and be mindful of letting water or moisture collect and fester. Common places where mold hides are in the bathroom, around the refrigerator, under sinks, around the shower and bathtub, in and around washing machines and dishwashers, around windows, and in attics, basements, and subflooring.

Dust regularly: Dust can contain bacteria, carcinogens, dead skin cells, dander, dirt, dust mites and their feces, flame retardants, heavy metals, insect parts, mold spores, PFOA, PFOS, phenols, pollen, viruses, VOCs, and more. In recent studies, most household dust that was tested

contained phthalates as well. Use a damp cloth or microfiber cloth to wipe down surfaces at least once a week for immediate and sustained improvement in your indoor air quality.

Let in light: Bacteria, mold, and other nasty things thrive in the dark. Opening the shades and letting light flood in can help keep the inside of your home healthier. It has also been shown to improve mood and energy.

Minimize clutter: Less clutter means fewer places for dust and all that's in it to become trapped. It also makes it much easier to keep the home and the air in it cleaner and less toxic.

No shoes inside: Shoes bring in many things from their travels we really don't want in our homes. This includes much more than dirt. (Yes, stuff like fecal matter, and lots of it.) One study by microbiologist Dr. Charles Gerba found 96 percent of shoes had fecal matter on the outside and are dirtier than a toilet seat. Other unwanted house guests include bacteria and viruses, fungi, gasoline, heavy metals, herbicides and pesticides, and mold. Leave the shoes at the door. There's a great amount of health benefit to walking barefoot, too (see page 157).

Open windows: Every day, open your windows (and even doors!) for at least 10 minutes. Twice a day is even better.

Replace HVAC filters: These, often, are forgotten and replaced much less frequently than they should be. Most manufacturers recommend replacing filters every ninety days, and even sooner for those who struggle with allergies. The 3- to 4-inch (7.5 to 10 cm) filters at the main unit typically need to be replaced every six to nine months. A MERV 13 filter or better is the standard recommendation. Set a reminder on your phone, write it in your calendar, or use a company that offers a subscription service that will send the replacement filters at the recommended intervals, reminding you to update yours.

Use fewer toxic cleaning supplies: Even while not in use, and stored away, cleaning supplies release VOCs and other toxic matter into the air. Swap them for homemade or healthier premade items (see page 71 for more on this).

Utilize ventilation fans: Ideally, you want one fan running over the stove when cooking and one running in the bathroom during, and for at least 20 minutes after, baths and showers.

Vacuum regularly with a sealed HEPA filter-equipped vacuum: Vacuuming will help limit dust, as well as other dirt and fibers that collect on surfaces. A HEPA filter will capture smaller particulate matter and prevent it from being released back into the air. A vacuum that uses sealing technology will trap the dust and allergens inside and further prevent that dirty air from reentering your home.

Go Further, When Finances Allow

Deep clean: A good deep clean includes washing walls, cleaning behind furniture, washing curtains, and getting to those forgotten spaces. Create a rotating schedule so you get to one of these tasks every couple of months. I've found this makes it less overwhelming and still ensures that everything gets a good deep clean a couple times a year.

Get air ducts cleaned: Most experts suggest this should be done at least every three to five years. You may want to do it even more frequently in older homes, homes with pets, and homes where people with allergies or respiratory problems reside.

Invest in a quality air filter: Big-box store models can help and typically utilize HEPA filtration. There are higher-quality models available that will capture particulate one hundred times smaller than a HEPA can or better, but these are typically special-order items. Some things to look for in a quality air purifier:

- Choose HEPA filter or better. HEPA can filter particulate matter 0.3 micron or larger. Some units filter down to 0.003 micron in size, capturing matter one hundred times smaller than a HEPA filter alone can, which means some filters will capture more particulate matter in the air than others.

- Charcoal or carbon filter layers can reduce or remove more pollution from smoke, odors, and fumes including VOCs.

- Sealed systems prevent captured air from escaping the unit and recirculating back into the air.

- Consider the cost of ownership and not just the initial investment. How often do filters need to be replaced? What do replacement filters cost? How much electricity is used running the filter? Is there a warranty? How long might this unit last with proper use and upkeep? Some filters may cost less initially but more than another in the same performance range over time.

Mold inspection, remediation, and maintenance: Proper mold inspection and testing can be pricey. Remediation can be as well. Yet, these steps can make a huge impact in the health of your home and for its inhabitants. Thoroughly research any inspector or team you may hire well before making this investment.

Walls, Furniture, Floors, and More

Following are some tips for tackling these large spaces and items found in all homes.

Walls

I'm not addressing all of the materials used to make the walls in your home here, but I'll share a few options to get you started in case you have a home renovation project on your list. Hot tip: Wool is a fabulous insulation material! Its nontoxic, works great, is naturally flame retardant without chemicals, helps absorb and regulate indoor air contaminants, prevents critters and mold, and more. There are a number of other eco-friendly options for insulation available, too. For drywall, some good options include natural gypsum board and USG Sheetrock. Look for terms like VOC-free and GREENGUARD Gold Certified. Hardwood that is unfinished, untreated, and natural is a great option for woodwork, like window framing, trim, and doors.

Paints and Stains

A freshly painted room might seem harmless, but most paints contain chemical compounds that can impact our health long after the fresh paint smell fades. Every year, it seems like there are more paints with safer ingredients becoming available thanks to awareness, and demand, increasing.

Many of these paints are very high performing. Those I've used have actually performed much better than the conventional paints I was used to! For primers, paints, and stains, a great place to start is to look for paints that list low to no VOCs in the base as well as the colorant. APE Free is another helpful qualification. Alkylphenol ethoxylates, or APEs, are chemicals used as surfactants in some paints that can contribute to reproductive issues and hormonal disruption. Benzene/glycol, heavy metals, and antimicrobials are other items to look out for in paint.

Furniture

For wood items, plywood and manufactured woods tend to use a lot of adhesives and other materials that are high in VOCs, like benzene, formaldehyde, and vinyl acetate. For furniture, fewer glues typically means less toxins. When replacing pieces in the home, some things I avoid, when possible, are manufactured woods, pieces that clearly use adhesives, plastics, and painted and varnished/finished woods. Less-toxic options include furniture made of solid hardwoods that are unfinished or finished using natural materials like beeswax, or oils like linseed or walnut.

For upholstered items, some things to be mindful of are adhesives, fillings, flame retardants, and treatments such as stain-resisting or water-wicking chemicals. Some healthier options for fillings for chairs and sofas include organic latex, wool, and CertiPUR-US®–certified foam. More options are becoming available with organic or otherwise healthier upholstery materials and dyes as well. Some furniture makers utilize third-party testing, such as OEKO-TEX® and GREENGUARD Gold, to ensure the products are A Little Less Toxic. Some common furniture manufacturers are taking steps to ensure low to no VOCs in furniture options and may make claims like "certified nontoxic"—but it's important to dig beneath the marketing claim and make sure you get what you pay for. IKEA, a Swedish-based company, has a pretty sophisticated list of chemicals it does not allow in its furniture. This list includes banning BPA, brominated flame retardants, cadmium, lead, mercury, and PVC. It's important to read labels, looking for things such as formaldehyde in items like foam as well as fluorinated or water-repelling chemicals.

If buying less-toxic, usually more expensive, furniture is not an option, you can help speed up the off-gassing process a bit. After bringing the piece home, when possible, take the furniture outside into the fresh air and sunshine. The sun can help accelerate the off-gassing, and being out in the open air means fewer VOCs and air contaminants will enter your home. Bring the piece in at night so it doesn't accumulate moisture and damage the furniture or encourage mold growth. If possible, the garage or other less-used shelter space is a great place to store the furniture overnight. Putting it out again for another day or two when and where you can, as weather permits, can make a positive difference for your home's air quality and environment. Another option could be to keep the furniture in a room with an air purifier, or move the air purifier to the room with the new furniture. Keeping the windows open as much as possible can help the off-gassing chemicals escape instead of being trapped in the room and home.

Buying secondhand furniture can greatly reduce the amount of off-gassing, which usually happens when items are newer. However, older furniture can include mold and wood rot or other materials and fillings, and upholstered pieces can break down, potentially polluting the air. Be alert, too, for things like bedbugs and fragrances and odors.

Organic cotton, linen, and wool make great cover options. Polyfill of any variety means plastic. Healthier fill options include buckwheat, flax, kapok, organic cotton, untreated feathers, and wool. This is another area where certifications like OEKO-TEX®, CertiPUR-US®, GOTS, etc., can be very helpful when making buying decisions.

When it comes to decor, I'm not going to cramp your style here. I just want to give you a few tools and some things to keep in mind as you make your space beautiful and uniquely yours. Be mindful of clutter. It bears repeating. Clutter makes it harder to keep the air in your home healthy. Items that rank higher on the toxin list include those made with cadmium, lead, manufactured wood, and plastic and with strong chemical paints and varnishes. Less-toxic options typically include beeswax candles, ceramics and pottery made with natural materials, glass vases or other items, solid wood, woven baskets of natural materials like jute or hyacinth, organic throw pillows or blankets, and other natural textiles.

Cozy Things and Decor

Much to my husband's dismay, I'm a sucker for throws and pillows. I try to keep it to a minimum, out of my respect for him and his sincere disdain for throw pillows as well as my desire to limit clutter and dust, but I'm not giving them up. Organic cotton and bamboo are great materials for throw blankets. For throw pillows, I appreciate a removable cover I can wash regularly to manage dust.

Floors

This is a common place to find adhesives, resins, VOCs, and other contributors to indoor air pollution hiding. Flooring to avoid includes laminate, man-made linoleum, manufactured wood, and most vinyl.

The best nonwood options include natural laminate, natural and unsealed stone, some bamboos and vinyls, tile (with low-tox grout), and unsealed, unstained concrete. Look for certifications like GREENGUARD Gold or testing for VOCs to show low to no traces of these chemicals. The best wood options include unfinished hardwood. You can stain and seal it yourself with less-toxic options, if needed.

When it comes to carpets and rugs, I prefer to forgo carpet, when possible. It traps dust and everything else that comes with it and can harbor mold and mycotoxins. It's also expensive to choose less-toxic carpeting. Most is made with synthetic materials, which are made from plastic petrochemicals such as polypropylene, which is toxic on its own and can off-gas for years. In addition, they tend to be coated with or woven with biocides, flame retardants, petrochemicals, PFAS-containing stain repellents, phthalates, surfactants, and VOCs that will continuously off-gas into the air (and sometimes increase in toxicity over time as the fibers wear down). Even the dyes used can

pose potential problems as they can contribute to the overall off-gassing and can contain heavy metals and other VOCs. Carpeting is often glued to the floor using toxic glues. As with any other thing I'm writing about, if you have carpet, please don't panic. Enjoy that squishy coziness on your feet! This information is here for anyone who wants to know more about what is in their home and what can be a healthier alternative when and if the time comes to make a swap.

My preference when you need the coziness that carpet can provide is to opt for area rugs made with natural fibers. Wool is a wonderful alternative to many synthetic rug materials as it is sustainable, soft, and durable, while being a healthier choice, too. Other natural fibers that can be a less-toxic yet still beautiful way to add texture and cozy up any room include cotton, denim, hemp, jute, or sisal. Natural dyes are a great option, when accessible.

I'm more cautious about the use of cotton due to its reputation as "the world's dirtiest crop" (see page 84 for more). Cotton accounts for a little more than 2 percent of the world's cultivated land, yet nearly 25 percent of insecticides and more than 10 percent of pesticides used worldwide go toward growing cotton crops. Yikes. If I need to shop for a cotton rug or other cotton textile, I try to find organic cotton that fits my needs and budget. That's not always easy to do, so I lean toward other natural fibers instead.

I always look for rugs without any backing because rug backing is attached to the rug with strong adhesives that have plenty of ingredients I'd rather keep out of my home, including formaldehyde. That stuff. Again. It shows up in so many places in the home we may often not think of and that's exactly why limiting it when and where we can makes a big impact. Most rug descriptions detail whether there is a backing included. If checking in person, just turn that bad boy over and take a look. On a rug without backing, you should be able to see a reverse side of the very pattern you see on the top side of the rug. If you want a cushioning pad or anti-slip pad under the rug, natural rubber, silicone, or wool works well for that task.

For those who love a full, carpeted area, there are some options that use natural fibers like wool and healthier

backings like latex and refrain from using chemical moth and stain repellents or flame retardants. There are also a few options for synthetic carpeting tested for VOCs, but most still use chemical treatments for things like stain prevention, odor neutralizing, and flame retardants. Ask questions and get to know what you're spending your hard-earned money on and inviting into your home and air, possibly for many years.

Miscellaneous Materials

Adhesives, caulks, and glues: These products are used all over the home in many areas. Little bits add up fast when used in so many places and they can be a source of many of the ingredients we are trying to minimize in our homes. When looking for a less-toxic option, avoid ingredients like biocides, BPA, ethylene glycol, formaldehyde, isocyanates, phthalates, styrene, and talc. There are brands that offer effective choices for each category here with low or no VOCs.

Cabinetry: Just like other wood in the home, solid wood is best here for a healthier, low-tox option. This option isn't always easy to come by or very budget friendly, so when it comes time to replace or update, some options can include using as much hardwood as possible, using less-toxic paints, stains, and sealers, and replacing cabinets with solid wood shelves in some areas. For cabinet elements made of manufactured wood, you can use some sealers like a safecoat to help prevent off-gassing. For cabinet hardware, I recommend wood, some metals, or natural stone.

Counters: For bathrooms, kitchens, and elsewhere, healthy counter materials include concrete, solid wood, or natural stone like limestone, marble, or quartzite sealed with a no- or low-VOC finishing sealant. Other healthy options include man-made quartz, like Cambria quartz, which has GREENGUARD Gold certification, or stainless steel.

Fixtures, sinks, and faucets: Investigate your options for truly lead-free materials. Stainless steel can be a great option for plumbing fixtures and other fixtures throughout the home. Ceramic, natural stone, and porcelain are great materials for sinks and tubs when using lead-free and safer sealers and finishes.

Lighting: Some lighting emits more blue light, which can be problematic for our sleep and health. Some also emits more EMF or "dirty electricity." Many times, these are one and the same. Fluorescent and CFL (compact fluorescent light) lightbulbs tend to emit the most blue light as well as the most EMF radiation, and they also may contain mercury. LED bulbs tend to emit plenty of blue light and EMF as well, however they typically emit less of both than CFL or other fluorescent bulbs. Incandescent bulbs are the

oldest type and although they're not as energy efficient, they emit warmer hues and less blue light and fewer EMFs. Sunlight is the best light; when we need light when the sun is gone, candles are the best. For electrical lighting, incandescent is my top choice, but it's becoming harder to find and some states don't even allow it to be shipped there.

EMF Protection

"EMF" stands for "electric and magnetic fields" or "electromagnetic fields." There are three types of EMF: electric field, magnetic field, and radio frequency radiation. EMF has always existed and always will. The Earth has a magnetic field generated from its very core. We are always in Earth's magnetic field and it is the reason compasses work and that creatures like ducks and fish are able to navigate to other places. Lightning during a storm creates a current between the sky and the ground, and that current is surrounded by an electromagnetic field. EMFs are also generated by many things that make modern technology and communication possible. Wi-Fi routers, power lines, microwaves, medical technology like MRI, and cell phones are all known for their contribution to EMFs.

EMFs are also generated by many other things we don't commonly associate them with, such as:

- Anything Bluetooth-equipped or wireless, such as wireless speakers and headphones
- Baby monitors
- Breaker panels
- CD and DVD players
- Cell towers
- Clock radios/other radios
- Digital watches
- Electrical heaters
- Electrical wiring; electric panels and outlets
- Electric blankets
- Fluorescent and halogen lighting
- Hair dryers
- Induction cooktops
- Infrared heaters and saunas
- Laptops and computer monitors
- Printers
- Refrigerators and other electrical appliances
- Smart meters, smart TVs, or anything "smart"
- Under-the floor heating
- Ungrounded electronics
- Video game stations

Essentially, if it uses electricity or sends or receives information or data through broadcast waves, it generates EMF. Some objects emit more than others. The type of EMF, proximity to the source, and cumulative exposure may make individual differences.

Should we be concerned? Many believe the answer is yes, but there's no broad agreement on how concerned to be. For example, the World Health Organization listed cell phone radiation as a probable carcinogen in 2011 and has not made any updates since that time. Yikes. Studies are

being conducted and the current data is inconsistent. The conclusion is, typically, that certain EMF radiation "may" contribute to or cause X, Y, or Z.

We cannot avoid all EMF exposure. Attempting to do so would create unreasonable amounts of stress, which is also bad. My personal approach to EMFs is to be mindful of what I invite in, mitigate where I can, and take care of my body in other ways I can control, like with good nutrition, movement, and rest.

Here is my strategy for a less-toxic home regarding EMFs:

- Limit the number of objects in the home that add to EMFs.

  ○ Anything "smart," anything using Bluetooth, etc. This includes TVs, monitors, thermostats, etc., and any unnecessary wireless technology, especially those that are in close proximity to or worn on the body.

  ○ Request that the local energy company swap out the smart meter attached to your home for older technology; many will do this for free or a small fee.

- Use the stovetop, toaster oven, electric pressure cooker, etc., to reheat and skip the microwave.

- Hardwire as much as possible.

- Turn off or unplug devices as much as possible.

  - Even when not "on," many appliances still emit EMF when not in use. Conserve energy and reduce EMF by unplugging things like the blender, etc., when not in use.

  - Turn off Wi-Fi at night, or use something like a light timer to automatically shut it off at preset times.

- Turn off broadcasting devices as much as possible. Even while not in active use, having Bluetooth or Wi-Fi switched on means the device is regularly transmitting signals searching for connections, which wears out batteries faster and increases EMF exposure.

  - Turn off Wi-Fi on cell phones and other devices when not in use and whenever possible.

  - Turn off all Bluetooth not actively being used.

  - Switch to "airplane mode" whenever possible.

- Create distance.

  - Keep your cell phone out of your pocket, when possible.

  - Avoid Bluetooth headsets and earbuds.

- Avoid smart watches or other devices worn against the body, or turn on airplane mode as much as possible.

- Avoid using the phone or laptop on your physical body, especially when they are plugged in.

- Use speakerphone, when possible, to avoid Bluetooth devices or holding the phone to your head. Wired headsets are typically a better choice, too. Some are made to reduce or eliminate radiation.

- Make the bedroom a safe haven.

  - You're in this space for one-third or more of your life. This is where rest and restoration take place. Make this an EMF-free zone as much as possible by keeping phones out or on airplane mode, keeping distance from Wi-Fi routers if not off, etc.

- Make your body more resilient.

  - Nourish it with whole foods and plenty of clean water.

  - Move regularly.

  - Get adequate and quality sleep.

  - Limit stress.

  - Limit consuming things that deplete, like inflammatory foods, alcohol, stressful TV or other media, etc.

- Ground your body (see page 157).

  - Get your bare feet or hands in contact with nature more regularly (see page 151 for more on this).

Cleaning

I absolutely love a clean home. Before learning about what was actually in my cleaning products, I was of the mind-set that the "cleaner" a house smells, the better. Once I discovered this wasn't necessary or wise, I went looking for alternatives. At the beginning of my journey to make my life and home less toxic, I started making all of my household cleaners myself. I found it easier than reading a ton of labels, only to become frustrated and deceived. I also loved that it was budget friendly and saved my family money. Since then, I have found some great commercial options, yet I continue to make many of my own cleaners because I enjoy it and it works. You can find all my cleaning supply recipes as well as tips and tricks in the kitchen chapter, starting on page 71.

Aroma

It is said that more than 85 percent of American homes have some sort of scent in use. Air freshener sprays, melts, plug-ins, powders, and scented candles are major contributors to indoor air pollution. The pleasant aroma often comes with a heavy serving of endocrine disrupting phthalates, VOCs, and other contaminants that pollute air in the home and the bodies of those who breathe it. This is unnecessary and presents a very simple way to make our home and bodies healthier: Stop using these items altogether, immediately. This wasn't easy for me. I love having a pleasant aroma in my home but I decided I don't need to spite my body for the sake of my nose. I still enjoy pleasant smells and have found a number of ways to add good aromas to my living space without compromising the quality of the air I breathe, or my health.

Candles can be problematic for a number of reasons. Most are made of paraffin and other petroleum-derived ingredients, and that alone can pollute the indoor air with additional chemicals like benzene and toluene. Soy candles are often no better. Add synthetic fragrance to any of these and they pollute your indoor air even when not being burned (see page 146 for more on candles). Here are some healthy, good-smelling home fragrance alternatives:

- Simmer pot: Simmer a pot of water on the stovetop, or use a slow cooker, with some good-smelling ingredients like apple slices, cinnamon sticks, clove, coconut pieces, cranberries, eucalyptus, grapefruit, lavender, lemon, lime, mint leaves, orange, pine sprigs, rosemary, strawberry slices, vanilla, etc. Mix and match, get creative, have fun. Keep an eye on the pot and add more water periodically as it will evaporate over time as it simmers.

- Clean with baking soda and/or vinegar to help absorb and remove unwanted odors.

- Use ventilation when cooking and afterward.

- Open windows regularly to help reduce unwanted smells and lingering odors.

- Dust and vacuum regularly.

- Change HVAC filters regularly.

- Diffuse essential oils.

- Use unscented beeswax candles as they can actually help purify the air by releasing negative ions and give that cozy candle vibe. If using scented candles, opt for those with healthy wax options, like beeswax and coconut, that are scented with safer plant-derived ingredients and/or essential oils.

- Make your own air freshener sprays or purchase those made without "fragrance" and with ingredients you can feel good about inviting into your home.

- Move stinky items outside to freshen up in the fresh air and sunshine.

- Spray stinky upholstered items lightly with rubbing alcohol or vodka to eliminate odors.

DIY Air Freshener

My favorite combination of essential oils is included in this spray, but experiment to find your favorites as well. The witch hazel, or alcohol, helps neutralize odor as well as increases the speed of drying, so spots aren't left on fabric after being sprayed. I do not measure. It's not a perfect science. And it works. And it smells amazing. And it is not harmful to your health. Any spray bottle works, but I prefer the continuous mist kind for this.

Directions

In a 16-ounce (480 ml) spray bottle, combine the salt and essential oils. Add the witch hazel, then fill the bottle with distilled water. Cover, shake, and spray. Aaaaaahhhhh . . .

- ½ teaspoon salt
- 15 drops lemon essential oil (antibacterial, deodorizing, mood brightening)
- 10 drops orange essential oil (mood enhancing)
- 5 drops bergamot essential oil (can help with anxiety, deodorizing)
- 2 drops tea tree essential oil (disinfecting, soothing)
- 2 tablespoons (30 ml) witch hazel, rubbing alcohol, or pure vodka
- Distilled or filtered water

the **Kitchen** *and* **Food**

Have you ever noticed at most events or gatherings in the home, people tend to congregate in the kitchen? This space has become the hub of most homes. It's not just where food is stored, prepared, and served but it's also where memories are made and so many conversations are had. In the kitchen, you'll also find spices, food storage, utensils and cookware, serveware, drinking water, cleaning products, drinking vessels, and more. This space is a zone of great impact. Making this room a healthier place will contribute to a healthier home and a healthier life.

In this chapter, I begin with the first thing I think of when I think about the kitchen: food! There is truth in the saying "food is fuel" but it's so much more. Real food, by its very nature, is designed to nourish, fuel, restore, and heal and it has effects down to the cellular level of our bodies. In fact, I think food is so important that it will make up about half this chapter! The rest of the kitchen is about a room where we can make a big impact over time. Many changes made here can be simple, yet powerful. So, in the remainder of the chapter, we'll get into everything else, from what to watch out for when buying pots, pans, and utensils for the kitchen to the best ways to clean and maintain this important room. Let's get cooking!

Food

Just a few generations ago, nearly all food was untouched by modern pesticides and could be considered what we think of today as organic. Ingredients came from whole foods. Animals were raised on pastures, consuming their natural diets of grasses, insects, etc. They had regular access to sunshine and fresh air and plenty of time and space to move their bodies.

In a relatively short period of time, humans have become quite distant and disconnected from the way we previously gathered, prepared, and consumed food. Although we can't fully understand the potential ramifications of these changes, we are learning more about the consequences of a kitchen full of highly processed convenience products, full of ingredients our great-grandparents' bodies had never encountered. We are, in many ways, part of an experiment. The air, animals, plants, soil, water, and more are all affected by modern industrialized food practices. What we consume can have an impact, not just on us, but on the world. It makes a difference in our homes, but also our neighborhoods, and our world, when we buy foods that are better for the planet.

When inviting food into my home, I return to some of my fundamentals:

- Read the label and ingredients on everything.

- As an item wears out or runs low, research a better alternative within your means.

- Do not wait until something is completely gone before looking for a replacement that is A Little Less Toxic.

In addition to this, for food, I try to consider whether the ingredients are items that will nourish or deplete. There is not much gray area between these boundaries and I aim to have more things that nourish than things that can deplete in my refrigerator, pantry, and body.

Although I can share what I have done, I encourage everyone to do what makes sense for your unique circumstances, abilities, and finances. When I learned that specific ingredients were causing me physical pain, I removed all items containing those ingredients from my environment immediately. Some were given away or donated, and others were thrown away. For foods that contained ingredients I learned weren't nourishing me, I replaced them little by little over time as I used up what I had left. If it is within your means and you have a desire to purge and do a complete overhaul, I support that. We dispose of the food items that do not

serve us either in our bodies or in the garbage can or elsewhere. If that is not a reasonable approach for you, replace one product at a time, as you run low, with something containing better ingredients within your budget.

On the topic of budget: I hear so often that it is just too expensive to eat organic or buy whole foods. My husband and I were newly married and living on one income in an expensive city *and* paying off student debt when I

began this journey. I have learned how to make this approachable within many budgets. As with any item entering the home, it's important to read labels. (For more on this, refer to page 48.) Know what's going into your cart because, if it's entering your home, it's going to end up in your body. I opt for quality over quantity. Making this shift has made my home and body healthier and, in the long term, has helped my budget as well.

When to Buy Organic

Up until a few decades ago, all food was, essentially, organic. The ingredients lists for foods would have all been just whole foods. It's not unreasonable to view what we're living through as a form of an experiment—one we did not sign up for. We can opt out, to some extent, by filling our pantries, refrigerators, and ultimately our bodies with healthier choices, like organic foods. My philosophy on organic foods is, that's how food was meant to be. I like to say, "If you can, buy organic, and if you can't, don't panic." If you find me repeating that stress is toxic throughout this book, it's because there is no one-size-fits-all anything. We all have varied circumstances, seasons, and abilities. Oftentimes, the organic price is comparable to the conventional price, sometimes being different by just pennies, but not always.

My priorities for buying organic, when possible, include avoiding those items that are more heavily treated with antibiotics, hormones, pesticides and herbicides, and steroids or that are produced in unsanitary and inhumane living conditions. This includes dairy products, eggs, meat, poultry, and seafood, and most grains, nuts, and seeds. For buying produce, I appreciate tools like the Dirty Dozen and Clean 15 produced

by The Environmental Working Group (EWG) every year, listing produce items with the highest and lowest levels of pesticides that year. If buying all organic produce is not an option, buying organic from the Dirty Dozen list can be very helpful in reducing your exposure. In addition, genetically modified crops (GMOs) are often engineered to be able to withstand higher amounts of pesticides than before their modifications. For this reason, I prefer to buy organic when the particular produce item has a GMO version.

I also try to buy organic when it comes to processed or packaged goods. These items, like bars, chips and crackers, or boxed or canned soups, milks, and broths, and other snacks, can contain a wide variety of ingredients hiding in the ingredients list that I prefer to avoid–ingredients like artificial sweeteners, GMOs, high amounts of sugars, inflammatory oils, MSG, gums, dyes, and preservatives that I would rather not invite into my home or body. Buying these items as organic means they will not have artificial dyes, flavorings, preservatives, sweeteners, or GMOs, added hormones, glyphosate or other inorganic pesticides or chemicals, antibiotics, high fructose corn syrup, hydrogenated oils, or BHT/BHA.

the kitchen and food

10 Budget-Friendly Food Tips

1 Buy fewer packaged food items. Whole foods typically cost less than packaged foods and can be stretched much further.

2 Buy what's in season. Fruit or vegetables grown across the world are generally going to cost more because they have to be shipped via airplane, boat, train, truck, or by all, to get to your store.

3 Utilize tools such as the Environmental Working Group's Dirty Dozen to understand which produce items have the most exposure to pesticides to help determine which food items you will buy organic, if buying all organic is not in the budget.

4 Utilize frozen whole foods, such as berries, for smoothies, jellies, etc., or frozen vegetables for roasting or adding to soups, stews, and casseroles.

5 Buying some items in bulk can save money. I often shop bulk bins or retailers that sell in bulk for items that have long shelf lives, like beans, certain spices, lentils, peas, popcorn, quinoa, rice, salt, sweeteners, etc.

6 Shop around. Online apps and sites have made it easier to do some price-comparison shopping and also sale hunting. For some items, I wait for sales to make purchases and stock up accordingly. Some online markets have prices that match or beat local shops consistently.

7 Make use of that freezer! When I find good-quality meat on sale, I stock my freezer. Stored properly, meats can be kept frozen for months.

8 Eat out less. Eating out is almost always much more expensive than preparing food at home. Eating out even one or two fewer times a month makes a big difference in the budget, which can then be allocated to purchase better-quality food or other needs for the home.

9 Eat more plants. Meat can be a nourishing part of a balanced diet, yet eating meat at every meal is not the most sustainable way to eat well on a budget. My family prioritizes buying quality meat and we enjoy it fewer times per week.

10 Read the ingredient label before adding items to your cart. If you make a conscious choice to read and know what you're inviting into your home, you are going to be less likely to add items with fun labels and convenience foods that cost more and aren't as filling or nourishing.

The Pantry

I love to keep a well-stocked pantry. This helps me refrain from ordering out or struggling to put a nourishing meal together, even with little planning or preparation time. Having basic staples at the ready enables me to make a balanced and wholesome meal with whatever fresh meats, produce, or scraps I have on hand. What you keep in your pantry can contribute to a healthier home and a healthier you. I also enjoy hosting and feeding others, so I try to remain ready for any extra guest(s) at a moment's notice, but that's a personal preference. This section covers the basics and how to stock and make swaps for a pantry that is A Little Less Toxic.

Here are some things I try to keep stocked in my pantry:

- Acids: aged balsamic vinegar, red wine and white wine vinegars, rice vinegar, unpasteurized apple cider vinegar

- Condiments:
  - Coconut aminos, a great alternative to soy sauce, especially for those who don't tolerate soy or gluten well
  - Fish sauce without sugar, MSG, or preservatives; only anchovies and sea salt
  - Hot sauces made with only whole food ingredients
  - Mayonnaise made with avocado, coconut, or olive oil and whole food ingredients
  - Mustard without oils, sugars, or other additives
  - Organic ketchup with only organic sugar or no added sugars
  - Salad dressing: I make my own dressings and marinades but if you want to keep some in your pantry, look for those with whole food ingredients and that use better oils like olive, coconut, or avocado, and without artificial sweeteners or mystery ingredients like "natural flavors" or "artificial flavors."
  - Tahini with the only ingredient being sesame seeds
  - Worcestershire sauce without natural flavorings or other mystery ingredients

- Dried goods:
  - Collagen and gelatin powders from pasture-raised, grass-fed cows
  - Dried medicinal berries and herbs like clove, goji berry, kombu, star anise, etc.
  - Dried pasta with minimal and whole food ingredients

- Grains, legumes and beans, nuts, and seeds:
  - Grains: organic groats or rolled or steel cut oats without added ingredients

- Legumes and beans: dried, like split peas; adzuki, black, cannellini, kidney, lentils, pinto beans

- Nuts: raw and plain, including almonds, Brazil nuts, cashews, macadamia, pecans, pine nuts, and walnuts; nut butters with organic, raw nuts or seeds and no added ingredients

- Seeds: chia, flax, hemp, pumpkin, quinoa

- Meats and seafood: pasture-raised, grass-fed jerky; pasture-raised poultry in cans or jars; wild-caught anchovies, oysters, salmon, sardines, tuna

- Oils/fats: avocado oil, extra-virgin olive oil, ghee, tallow, toasted sesame oil, unrefined virgin or extra-virgin coconut oil

- Pantry produce: garlic, onions, potatoes, and sweet potatoes; keep onions separate from potatoes as they can make each other perish faster.

- Seasonings and dried herbs: No kitchen is complete without salt and pepper. Choose a good-quality unrefined sea salt without anticaking agents or any other added ingredients. Common table salts sometimes even have sugar hiding in them. In addition, herbs and spices can make basic ingredients taste better, contain vitamins and minerals, and may offer health benefits. A well-stocked pantry might include:

- Basil: antibacterial, anti-inflammatory, antioxidant, heart health, immune support, liver function

- Cayenne and other hot peppers: antioxidant, cell health, circulatory support, digestive support, heart health

- Ceylon cinnamon: anti-inflammatory, antimicrobial, blood sugar regulation, circulatory health, eye health, cholesterol support

- Coriander: antibacterial, antioxidant, blood sugar regulation, detoxifying, heart health

- Cumin: anti-cancer properties, antioxidant, digestive health, immune support

- Garlic: blood pressure, cholesterol, heart health, immune health, sugar regulation

- Ginger: anti-inflammatory, digestive support

- Mustard: antioxidant, nervous system support, respiratory health

- Onion: antioxidant, digestion, heart health, supports healthy blood pressure and blood sugar levels

- Oregano: anti-inflammatory, antimicrobial, antioxidant, antiviral

- Paprika: anti-inflammatory, blood sugar and cholesterol regulating properties, eye health

- Parsley: antibacterial, antioxidant, bone, eye, and heart health support

- Rosemary: antimicrobial, antioxidant, digestion, mood support

- Sage: anti-inflammatory, antioxidant, brain support

- Thyme: antibacterial, antioxidant, lung health

- Turmeric: anti-cancer properties, anti-inflammatory, antioxidant, heart health, memory health, mental health

- Sweeteners: coconut sugar, dried dates, dried or fresh fruits, pure grade B maple syrup, raw honey, unsulfured molasses

- Teas and coffee: Both can be sources of heavy metals, mold, mycotoxins, and pesticides. If consumed regularly, this may be an area to be more mindful of. I shop for organic teas and coffees because those are consumed daily in our home (sometimes multiple cups a day!). I also source brands that do third-party testing for other contaminants like those I mentioned. Loose leaf or tea crystals will ensure you're not inviting microplastics and other toxic materials into your body via tea bags. For tea in tea bags, avoid any in fancy shapes or that are shiny as those are typically higher in plastic content. Unbleached paper tea bags are, generally, the less-toxic option.

- Treats: fair-trade organic dark chocolate (at least 70 percent cacao)

A Note on Grains (and Beans and Nuts . . .)

Grains are the seeds of a plant. This means they are the part of the plant that contains all the information to grow . . . even years later. Because of this, they have numerous properties that help protect them from the environment so they can survive and make new plants. It's their job. This is true for beans, chia seeds, legumes, lentils, nuts, and rice! The protective properties include things like lectins and phytic acid and other constituents that not only protect the seeds from the environment but also can make them difficult for our human digestive system to break down. These compounds are often referred to as anti-nutrients as they make it difficult for our bodies to absorb, accrue, or process the nutrients the

grain contains. Traditionally prepared grains, which includes soaking before cooking, sprouting, and fermenting them, have a decreased amount of anti-nutrients, making the grain easier for the body to digest and also making the resulting grain higher in absorbable nutrients, thereby increasing its health benefits. A healthy gut is foundational to overall health, and properly preparing grains like with the traditional approach can be a great way to guard the gut. Properly prepared grains mean less gas and bloating, less gut disruption, and more nourishment.

I store dried organic grains, such as beans, in my pantry. At least one night before I plan to eat them, I pour a desired amount into a large glass bowl, cover with plenty of filtered water, at least by a couple of inches, and add about ¼ cup (60 ml) of an acid, typically apple cider vinegar. Others use lemon juice or another acid. I cover the bowl with a clean towel or a loose lid to prevent dust or other unwanted things from landing in the bowl and leave it on the counter for eight hours, or overnight. Then, I drain the liquid through a colander. I can then cook my beans and grains however I wish.

I also leave whole grains or beans to sprout for increased digestibility and greater health benefits when I have the time and ability. To sprout them in the colander, leave the grains (after soaking and draining) over a dish to catch any drips, loosely covered. You want air to be able to circulate but also keep out dust, etc. Leave the grains in a cool, dark place, if possible. Mine is usually on my kitchen counter. In the morning and before bed, pour clean water over the grains, still in the colander, to rinse them and keep them damp. Return to the sprouting place with the loose cover. Repeat until sprouts appear. Then eat, prepare, or cook the sprouted beans or grains however you like. Raw, sprouted lentils are great in a salad. Sprouted beans make the best chili that doesn't leave everyone stinking up the place afterward.

I often prepare more than I need of a grain and store extra in wide-mouth canning jars in my freezer. I just move a jar from the freezer to the refrigerator overnight, or the counter, and later a bowl of warm water to plop them out and heat up. This makes a great alternative to a can of beans. Did you know canned beans are almost never soaked or sprouted and they are almost always pressure cooked in the very can you buy them in? That can itself is a toxic material and is typically lined with BPA, BPS, or other materials known to be toxic and problematic for our health. Heating the can to a high temperature to cook the contents makes leaching of these ingredients into the food a higher likelihood, increasing the toxicity of the end product. Using beans I soak myself is also a money saver as dried beans and other grains are significantly lower in cost than canned. Save money, less toxic, better for your gut and health. Win, win, win.

Fermented Foods and Eggs

Although these items are more perishable, both are an important part of my pantry. For those who do not have histamine issues, fermented foods can be a fantastic source of probiotics or beneficial bacteria. One serving of a traditionally fermented food like kefir, kimchi, pickled cucumber, sauerkraut, yogurt, etc., can have greater probiotic diversity with many more specific strains of beneficial bacteria and up to 110 times or more probiotics than any supplement.

Fermented food provides a significant cost savings over a pill or liquid supplement. Multiple jars of sauerkraut or fermented carrots can be made at home easily with water and salt for a couple of dollars and can last months. Even store-bought fermented foods are often much lower in cost than a supplement. Yep, you can get exponentially more beneficial bacteria at a fraction of the price. In addition, fermented foods may also have bioactive components that a supplement does not. Each bioactive component comes with its own unique list of health benefits that can include being antibacterial, antioxidant, detoxifying, and more. Fermented foods also can contain beneficial enzymes that support digestion and help the body absorb nutrients more easily. Even more, when a food is fermented, it may have increased nutritional content as well as decreased anti-nutrients, like phytic acid. Better on the budget, better bang for the buck, better benefit. A big win.

Okay, on to eggs, which are extremely nutrient dense, especially for their size. Eggs have more nutrients per calorie than most other foods. They are high in protein and are a good source of many vitamins and minerals—including choline, folate, iron, lutein, phosphorus, riboflavin, selenium, vitamins A, B^{12}, and D, and zinc. In addition, eggs contain multiple antioxidants, plenty of omega-3 fatty acids, and all nine essential amino acids, which are the building blocks of protein. All of this is what contributes to a long and growing list of ways eggs may contribute to better health, including improving cholesterol levels, contributing to heart health, stroke prevention, brain and eye health, and more.

Yet, eggs can also be a confusing item to purchase as packaging claims can be misleading. "Farm fresh" can mean many things. The "farm" may be a huge, overcrowded barn where the chickens have no room to walk and never see the sunshine. This is also true for terms like "all natural," "free range," and others you're likely

room to lie down. It should not be a surprise that the chickens that roam on pasture enjoying sunshine and fresh air, moving their bodies all day, and eating their natural diet are found to be healthier. The meat and eggs of pasture-raised hens are shown to have a higher nutrition content with almost two times as much vitamin A, two times more omega-3 fatty acids, three times more vitamin E, and seven times more beta-carotene than factory-farmed chickens.

So, when shopping for eggs, the terms that actually carry weight to me are "pasture raised" and "organic." If I have to pick one, I choose pasture raised. Better for the bird and better for me.

Note: For meats, pasture raised is best. Grass-fed and grass-finished beef and lamb, pasture-raised pork and poultry; same for dairy: pasture-raised, grass-fed, organic butter, cheese, and milk, raw, if possible; grass-fed and organic yogurt, sour cream, kefir, and cream.

familiar with. The way our food is grown, raised, and lives impacts its nutrition. What we eat matters and what we eat eats matters, too. Terms like "vegetarian fed" drive me bonkers. Chickens are not herbivores! In nature, chickens forage and roam in open air and sunshine and enjoy an omnivorous diet including grubs, insects, and worms. "Cage-free" chickens are typically confined in a large barn, indoors, without access to fresh air and sunshine in which to roam or their natural diet. Most of the time, these chickens are so tightly packed in, there may not even be

Produce

Not much can beat fresh, whole foods when it comes to nourishment. Produce is a key component of my diet, which means I keep plenty of fresh produce on hand but aim not to purchase more than we can reasonably use before it rots. Local and in season is best.

THE WASH

My A Little Less Toxic produce wash that I've been using for almost a decade has been shared many, many times by people all over the place, and is a low-cost and effective way to easily clean produce. It serves a few purposes, though, and is used for conventional as well as organic produce.

As soon as fresh produce enters my home, I clean most of it: I fill a clean sink with cool water and about 1 cup (240 ml) or so of organic white vinegar. Vinegar can reduce mold by up to 80 percent, reduce parasites, and is antibacterial, antifungal, and antimicrobial. I add most of my fresh produce to the wash and let it soak for a while. Yes, even items I don't eat the skin of like bananas and lemons. (I'll explain shortly!) Soft-skinned items, like peaches and pears, I only leave for a minute or two. Harder, thicker-skinned items like avocado, bananas, and citrus I let soak for about 10 minutes as I'm sorting and storing the rest of my groceries.

Items I do not soak are those that need to be dried before coming to market or with many crevices and folds, like cabbage, garlic, onions, potatoes; instead, I rinse these items before use, as needed. I have no concern for or fear of dirt.

All produce has a story. It lived in the ground or on a plant and was exposed to nature and the elements, including animal matter, environmental toxins, fungi, mold, etc. It was picked by hand or machine and transported in receptacles to trucks, boats, and/or trains. During transport, it was likely exposed to exhaust and other environmental toxins. It was put on a shelf or in a bin and potentially touched by many hands. So, as it enters my home, it is immediately cleaned. This cleaning also helps preserve the life of the food as it can minimize molds and fungi that may be taking up residence on the items. After the soak, all items are laid out on clean towels to air-dry as long as needed. Everything must be completely dry before storing to help minimize bacterial and mold growth. All items are then stored appropriately.

STORAGE

Pay attention to how produce is displayed in the store. However you find the item at the market is typically the best way to store it at home. If it's refrigerated at the store, keep it

refrigerated at home. If it's kept out at room temperature, it's usually best to do the same at home. For example, tomatoes are always kept at room temperature at the store. They lose a ton of flavor when refrigerated. Onions, potatoes, and garlic reside in the pantry where it's cool and dark like their familiar home, the ground. As I mentioned earlier, I keep onions and potatoes separated; they make each other age faster. Contrary to my own rule, though, I keep citrus and apples in the refrigerator because the cooler temperature can help them last longer without impacting flavor too much.

Now, avocados have a reputation for having about a one-day window of perfect ripeness. I have a great tip to make that window a whole lot bigger! I let my avocados ripen on the counter with my other countertop produce. Once I can feel that perfect little bit of give when I press an avocado, I move it to the refrigerator. This extends that perfect ripeness window by days, and even up to a couple of weeks, in my experience. I can reach in and grab a perfectly ripe avocado almost anytime with this trick. I do the same with other stone fruits, like nectarines and peaches. Yes, avocado is a fruit. A stone fruit.

The Freezer

My freezer stays stocked with a few items I can use at a moment's notice to pull together a quick jam, smoothie, cough elixir, side, meal, or dessert. Some things my freezer typically contains are:

- Flax-filled cloth-covered eye pillows. Okay, not food related, but we use these for all the little bumps and bruises that happen daily with two little ones running around. These make great "ice packs." Our freezer always has a few ready for action.

- Homemade bone broths in canning jars or silicone cubes or bags

- Meats (stock up on sale)

- Organic berries and chopped fruits, like mango and pineapple

- Organic vegetables like broccoli, chopped spinach, peas, riced cauliflower

- Portioned out, nourishing, home-cooked meals from double-batch cooking

- Soaked and/or sprouted and cooked beans or lentils

- Wild-caught fish like Alaskan salmon, Atlantic cod, and scallops

Supplements

Remember, supplements are just that, a supplement to your diet. They are not meant to replace delicious fresh foods. The goal should always be to meet your nutritional needs with food and nature first. When a need can't be reasonably met, look for supplements with whole food ingredients, or safer synthetics without fillers and binders. There are more and more brands making these easier to find. It's also important to keep in mind we are all bio-individual with needs that change and it's not wise to follow anyone else's protocol. Appropriate lab work can be

a beneficial tool to determine what is a good fit for you. As with all things, read those ingredients and make informed decisions.

Pots, Pans, and Bakeware

I admit, my own kitchen had tons of nonstick cookware in it until I began to learn about the potential dangers of the materials used to make things "nonstick." Virtually all nonstick cookware contains PFAS (polyfluoroalkyl substances) like perfluorooctanoic acid, also known as PFOA. In recent years, more and more research is emerging demonstrating links from these nonstick materials to many ailments and diseases. The Centers for Disease Control (CDC) says, "PFAS may affect reproduction, thyroid function, the immune system, and injure the liver" and, in studies, found PFAS in the serum of all people tested. The American Cancer Society lists PFOA as a potential risk as it is persistent in the environment and the human body and has been found in virtually everyone's blood all over the world.

What's more, when I started seriously looking into my pans, I discovered that many of those that weren't nonstick were mostly aluminum, another material with potential toxicity concerns and connections to health issues, including Alzheimer's and other diseases. The chemicals used to form these materials don't remain in the pan. When our cookware is heated, especially at higher temperatures, the chemicals can leach into the food we

then eat. They may also be released into the air we breathe and enter the water system and, thus, the water we drink.

Although there is some debate, many believe nonstick cookware should be replaced every few years due to scratching and chipping, which means the coating can be introduced to foods cooked in it. This makes owning this type of cookware a more costly investment, especially over time.

My top choices for healthier cookware are materials that are nontoxic and will last for decades, or longer. (I have a wild dream that my children will have to debate who gets which of Mommy's pans when I'm no longer here!) With that in mind, here are some of my recommendations.

Stainless-Steel Pans

Stainless steel is typically going to have an aluminum core at the base, as that is a good conductor of heat. Stainless steel on its own is not a good heat conductor and a solid stainless pan is going to have cold spots and burn spots. You don't want a pan that's hotter in some spots than others! Even heat distribution will help you be a better cook. Because I try to mitigate and avoid aluminum exposure, I look for stainless-steel cookware that is

Cast-Iron Pans

three- to five-ply clad. This means there are layers of stainless and other materials covering the aluminum and providing a protective barrier between it and your food. I look for pans that are clad all the way up the sides as well. Some products are called "clad base," or something along those lines, indicating the extra layers are only at the bottom of the pan. Most of us can't simply cook all food (think pasta sauce) only at the bottom of a pan, so clad up the sides is important. I also look for 18/10, indicating the chromium to nickel ratio, respectively. Although 18/8 is also good, nickel helps prevent stains, rust, and corrosion, and helps retain shine. That means 18/8 will not hold polish long and 18/0 will not resist rust or corrosion well.

After a little practice and a ride on the learning curve, I can cook eggs and virtually anything in my stainless pans without sticking or any intense cleanup.

Note: A low-tox and very inexpensive stainless pan cleaner and polisher found easily is Bon Ami. Get some. Trust me. Also great for sinks, potties, tubs, and more.

This multipurpose pan can be used for decades of cooking. In fact, a single pan will last a lifetime, and beyond, if cared for properly. You can, of course, buy used cast-iron pans and restore them until they are as good as new. For what it's worth, I find my cast iron the easiest pan I have to cook in and clean. When shopping for a cast-iron pan, look for those pre-seasoned with less-toxic oils like flaxseed oil, if possible. Many are pre-seasoned with oils including vegetable, sunflower, and grapeseed. This is not a deal breaker to me, but may be for some. (I will clean my pan and season it with my own oils at home and will replace the less-favorable oils pretty quickly with use.)

In addition to cast iron, enameled cast iron is another great option. It has a nonporous surface, it's naturally nonstick, and it doesn't require any "seasoning" like traditional cast iron does. The enamel can protect the iron from rust and make a pan more durable. The enamel layer also prevents leaching of iron into food, for those looking to limit iron. Most enameled cast-iron cookware is safe for use on the stovetop and in the oven up to 450°F or 500°F (232°C or 260°C).

CAST-IRON TIPS

To season: While most new pans come "pre-seasoned," I like to get my pans as clean and nonstick as possible before cooking in them.

1 Wash with warm soapy water.

2 Dry well.

3 Using a soft, clean cloth, apply a thin layer of flaxseed oil to the pan. Oils like coconut can work, too, but flaxseed seems to create a nice hard "shell" for the foundation that helps make the pan nice and slick and nonstick.

4 Bake the pan, upside-down with a pan placed underneath it to catch any drips, in a 325°F (163°C) oven for 1 hour. Let cool completely before removing from the oven.

5 Repeat a few times to get a stronger initial "seasoning" on your pan.

To use:

• Cook in the pan over low to medium heat for most things.

• Avoid using acidic ingredients, like tomato, in the pan, which can leach excess iron from the pan into the food. (Use another type of pan for those recipes.)

• Using cast iron often is enough to keep the pan well seasoned.

• Clean (see at right), dry, and store away from any moisture. If stacking and storing more than one item, place a protective layer between the pans, something as simple as paper towels, to avoid scratches that can promote rust.

To clean:

• Rust is your enemy! Make sure the pan is completely dry after cleaning and before storing.

• Do not use soap to wash the pan after that first initial cleaning. Soap will erode the precious layers of oils you've been working so hard to form and that make your pan amazingly nonstick.

• After normal use, simply wipe out your pan with a cloth or paper towel. Dry thoroughly and store in a cool, dry place.

• To remove caked-on gunk, use coarse salt or hot water and a sponge, brush, or stainless-steel chainmail. Rinse well. Then, heat the pan on the stove for a couple minutes. Rub on a very light coating of coconut oil. Let cool. Dry and store in a cool, dry place.

Baking, Mixing, and Measuring

For baking dishes, mixing bowls, measuring cups, food storage, and more, I often turn to glass. It's a reliable material and one that doesn't leach unwanted things into my food.

Ceramic is another great option for bakeware; if you're considering second hand or older items, ensure they are lead-free. Many colorful ceramic dishes, especially older ones, have been found to contain concerning levels of lead.

For baking sheets, stainless steel is my top choice. I try to follow the same guidelines when selecting these stainless products as listed earlier (see page 61). If you have aluminum or nonstick sheet pans you're not ready to part with, line them with unbleached parchment paper to create a barrier between the pan and your food.

General Kitchen Tips

1 Clean as you go. Small messes are less overwhelming and easier to manage than a giant mess at the end. Caked-on messes take longer to clean up. Mess is not a safe work environment, especially when knives, heat, and fire are involved.

2 A trash and/or scrap bowl at your work station is a good friend. This will save you time and help keep your prep area organized and safer to work in.

3 A sharp knife is safer than a dull knife. Dull knives require more pressure and allow more room for slips and mistakes that can turn dangerous.

4 A damp paper towel under your cutting board helps keep it safely in place for fewer accidents.

5 Aim for more homemade meals. They can save you money over time and are a great investment in your overall health.

6 Have fun! Food is fuel but it's also community, nourishment, culture, tradition, communication with the body, comfort, and more.

Tools and Gadgets

Anything you use in the kitchen, and especially items used regularly, should be evaluated as far as the materials are concerned. Choose new items (or replace old, worn-out ones) with less-toxic options.

Cooking appliances, such as air fryers, countertop convection ovens, toaster ovens, etc.: Many are coated with nonstick materials, but try to opt for those without them. A convection oven is essentially an air fryer. If you're in the market for one of these items, you may want to invest in a stainless countertop convection oven that can multitask, such as air fry, bake, roast, toast, reheat, all in one tool.

Cooking utensils, such as box grater and rasp grater, colander, funnels, measuring cups and spoons, mixing bowls, spatulas, spoons, whisks, etc.: I choose materials like glass, silicone, solid wood, and stainless for these items. (You're probably noticing a theme.) Even when materials are acceptable, I don't like items made with one piece glued to another—a silicone spatula with a wooden handle, for example. The tiny spaces where pieces connect can be a water trap and a place for mold and bacteria to fester—plus the glue!

Cutting boards: Opt for solid pieces of wood to avoid toxic glues. Wood is naturally antimicrobial. It requires a bit of care and maintenance but my wooden cutting boards have lasted a long time with minimal attention. I wipe or wash them after use and let dry thoroughly. Every couple of months I rub a little coconut oil across the surface of my boards to help keep them from absorbing too much moisture and to help keep the wood from cracking.

Pressure cooker: This is one of my most-used tools, as I like it not only to pressure cook, but also to slow cook, steam, and even reheat food in place of a microwave. My appliance is stainless steel on the inside with a silicone ring, but some brands use nonstick materials, so be mindful of that when shopping.

To reheat food with a pressure cooker, follow the manufacturer's instructions for your model. I usually add 1 cup

(240 ml) of water to the pot and place a trivet in it. I set my food in its glass or stainless container on the trivet, close and seal the lid, and select "Steam" or "Pressure Cook" for 0 minutes. In a few minutes or less, my food is perfectly reheated without making more dishes—or drying out or destroying delicate items like noodles or rice.

Storage containers: Glass, stainless, and food-grade silicone are my top picks for food storage containers. Plastic can leach chemicals into your food and it is not a sustainable material. Repurposed glass jars are a free way to make an upgrade from plastic. (I even freeze items in wide-mouth, straight-neck, canning jars . . . just leave room for expansion!) There are loads of options in every shape and size for glass containers and jars. If your household is addicted to plastic storage bags, try silicone instead.

Water Filtration

Municipal water is treated to limit
bacterial contaminants. In doing so,
toxic contaminants are used. Other
toxicants that enter the water system
through a variety of ways are not
filtered out before reaching your
tap. Municipal water is treated with
chlorine and, in many places still,
fluoride as well.

**Other contaminants commonly
detected in tap water include (but
are not limited to):**

Aluminum
Arsenic
Chromium
Disinfection byproducts
Lead
Pesticides
Prescription drugs
Radioactive materials

To check your tap water you can use the Environmental Working Group's Tap Water Database (ewg.org/tapwater), or send your well or tap water for analysis to companies like My Tap Score for reasonable rates.

A good water filtration system will greatly reduce or remove all of these substances and more. Options include countertop reverse osmosis or gravity-fed carbon filters, faucet attachments, pitchers, under-the-counter systems, and whole-house systems. Most are better than nothing. Use what's best for your budget and circumstances. (Don't forget to factor in the cost of replacement filters over time when determining what is best for your budget.) Other things to consider are the contaminants in your personal tap or well water, mineral removal, warranties, upkeep, and maintenance.

We currently have a gravity-fed countertop system we love. It is portable and does not require electricity, so it can be used in emergencies to turn virtually any water other than saltwater into safe drinking water. We even take it to vacation rentals and on camping trips so we have purified water anywhere. It removes more than two hundred contaminants, including pathogenic bacteria, pesticides, viruses, and multiple other toxicants.

And although the filter removes so much, it does allow minerals to be retained in the water, unlike other systems, such as reverse osmosis. Reverse osmosis systems can possibly remove even more potential contaminants, but also remove beneficial materials with them, requiring the user to account for this and add minerals back into the water before drinking it. Reverse osmosis systems also require excess water to produce purified water, resulting in using upward of 4 gallons of water (15 L) to produce 1 gallon (3.8 L) of purified water in some systems. I'm not against reverse osmosis. These are just some of the reasons we made the choice for the gravity-fed countertop unit and some factors to consider as you decide the best fit for your home. Ideally, I'd love to have a whole-house purification system that would retain the natural minerals in the water or add them back in. These systems do exist but can be pricey and usually require professional installation.

Cleaning Products

Many of the cleaning products we use in our homes are stored and used in the kitchen, so let's chat about them. If you've walked anywhere near a cleaning product aisle in any store, you can probably smell it right now as you're reading this. Think about that for a second. Those are sealed bottles and you can still smell their contents from a distance (and that's in a large, well-ventilated space). What is in our cleaning products affects the air we breathe. As I mention over and over, our homes' indoor air is often more toxic than outdoor air. Cleaning products are a big contributor to that condition even when they're not being actively used. I recommend swapping your cleaning products for less-toxic ones as soon as possible. For those you're not ready to replace or let go of, consider storing them in a sealed container outside or in a detached space such as a shed or garage. This simple change will instantly improve your indoor air quality and might help encourage you to make the swaps sooner (after a few trips outside).

When I first examined my cleaning products, I started out making most or all of them myself because it was less confusing to me than deciphering the labels and mile-long ingredients lists on the "supposedly" greener cleaners. It was also more budget friendly and

I found it fun! If DIY isn't your thing, there are store-bought and online options available. Look past marketing claims and fancy labels and look at actual ingredients.

Many products claiming to be nontoxic or less toxic contain ingredients I prefer to keep out of my home–ingredients that are known neurotoxins, endocrine disruptors, have studies linking them to diseases including cancer and respiratory illness, and more.

Some ingredients and claims to look out for include:

All natural or natural
Chlorine or bleach
Fragrance
Paraben
PEGs
Petrolatum and petroleum byproducts
Phenoxyethanol
Phthalates
Sodium laureth sulfate
Triclosan

Some of my tried-and-true DIY cleaning recipes are made with very common ingredients. With different combinations of these items, you can clean just about anything and everything—from the sink to the oven, countertops, toilet, tub, rugs, and more.

Some of my tried-and-true DIY cleaning recipes are made with very common ingredients. Different combinations of these items, you can clean just about anything and everything—from the sink to the oven, countertops, toilet, tub, rugs, and more.

The A Little Less Toxic DIY Cleaning Kit

- Arrowroot powder
- Baking soda
- Castile soap
- Hydrogen peroxide
- Isopropyl alcohol or vodka
- Lemons and lemon essential oil
- Microfiber cloths
- Old pillowcase
- Olive oil
- Repurposed jars
- Spray bottles
- White vinegar (Note: If you can find organic white vinegar, grab that, as white vinegar is made as a byproduct of corn, which is a GMO crop that is typically more heavily treated with pesticides.)

Simple DIY Recipes

ALLT Multipurpose Cleaner

This lemony-fresh multipurpose cleaner has been getting the job done in my home for years. The lemon breaks down dirt, grease, and grime; removes mineral deposits; lightens stains on surfaces, including grout; deodorizes; deters pests; combats rust; smells amazing; and is inexpensive. The vinegar also breaks down dirt, grease, and grime; dissolves mineral deposits; combats mold; is antibacterial and antifungal; absorbs odors then dissipates them; deters pests; and is inexpensive. Combining the two ingredients creates a powerful, yet healthy and gentle, cleaning agent for loads of uses around the home. It can get the job done without destroying the important microbiome of the home or polluting the indoor air.

Lemon-Infused Vinegar

- Lemon rinds, or other citrus rinds like grapefruit, lime, or orange
- White vinegar

Multipurpose Cleaner

- Filtered water

Directions

1 To make the lemon-infused vinegar: After using the juice of a lemon (or other citrus), pop the rinds in a large glass jar.

2 Cover the lemon rinds with white vinegar, making sure the rinds are submerged to help prevent mold growth. Cover the jar and let sit (I keep mine under the sink) for at least a couple weeks, but you can leave it for months. The lemons infuse the vinegar, making it more powerful and better smelling.

3 To make the cleaner: When ready to use, strain the infused vinegar through a fine-mesh strainer into a glass bowl. Discard the solids.

4 In a 16-ounce (480 ml) spray bottle, combine equal parts lemon-infused vinegar with filtered water and use as you would any multipurpose cleaner. Close. Shake. Spray. You can even combine some of the liquid with baking soda for a scrubbing paste.

STONE COUNTER CLEANER

Do not use my multipurpose cleaner, which contains vinegar, on granite or marble as the acid in the vinegar can damage those surfaces. To clean those materials, in a spray bottle, combine 3 tablespoons (45 m) rubbing alcohol and 1 teaspoon castile soap. Fill the rest of the bottle with filtered water. Close. Shake. Spray. Wipe.

Dusting Spray

"Dust" is a term used to describe an array of particles that collect together and land on surfaces. Dust is made up of organic and inorganic matter (see page 25 for more on this). Dusting is a great way to limit toxic exposures. Try to dust at least once a week. Microfiber is an excellent tool for this. A handy microfiber dusting wand makes the job very easy to make your space feel fresher and your body able to breathe easier.

- 2 tablespoons (30 ml) olive oil
- ¼ cup (60 ml) Lemon-Infused Vinegar (above)
- Filtered water

Directions

In a 12- to 16-ounce glass or steel spray bottle, combine the oil and vinegar. Fill the bottle with filtered water. Cover. Shake. Spray. Wipe. Sparkling-clean house.

DIY Sanitizer

Hand washing with soap and water is your best defense against germs. Oversanitizing is not my jam but there are times when this stuff is useful. If you keep a few simple ingredients "on hand," you can make this simple sanitizer easily and inexpensively.

I sometimes add an essential oil to the recipe. A few drops is plenty for a personal-size bottle of sanitizer. Some essential oils are even reported to have antimicrobial properties. They include cinnamon, eucalyptus, lavender, lemon, marjoram, peppermint, rosalina, spruce, tea tree, thyme, and oregano.

Keep in mind that to be effective, the final product should be at least 60 percent alcohol. Alcohol is very drying to the skin, so I like to add a little aloe to counter that. Depending on the type of alcohol you use, the ratios change. Here are some samples:

With 99% Isopropyl Rubbing Alcohol

- 2 parts alcohol
- 1 part aloe vera gel

With Everclear

- 2½ parts alcohol
- ½ part aloe vera gel

With 91% Isopropyl or Rubbing Alcohol

- 3 parts alcohol
- 1 part aloe vera gel

With 70% Isopropyl or Rubbing Alcohol

- 9 parts alcohol
- 1 part aloe vera gel

Directions

1 Choose the formula based on the type of alcohol you wish to use. The thicker formulas may work as a gel or a spray. The 70 percent formula is only going to work as a spray.

2 In a spray bottle or other container, combine the alcohol and aloe vera. Close. Shake. Use.

Note: If you're using vodka, the "proof" number is double the actual alcohol content. To reach a 60 percent or higher final alcohol content in your sanitizer, you need a very high proof vodka, like Everclear (190 proof = 95 percent alcohol).

Not all essential oils are recommended for use on or around children or people who may be pregnant or elderly.

Some aloe gels clump. I like the one by Beauty by Earth and have had good results with it.

DIY Stainless Appliance and Glass Cleaner

This cleaner costs cents to make and works great on glass and stainless-steel appliances. The alcohol helps the spray dry fast and limits streaking. It is nontoxic and lasts a long time. I use organic ingredients and purified water for my cleaning products, when possible, because it's another way to reduce toxic load and help make the home a little safer and A Little Less Toxic.

- ¼ cup (60 ml) white vinegar (preferably organic)
- ¼ cup (60 ml) isopropyl alcohol or vodka (preferably organic vodka, if using)
- Few drops lemon or orange essential oil (optional; but smells nice and helps with fingerprint removal)
- 1 tablespoon (8 g) arrowroot flour (also helps reduce streaking)
- Filtered water

Directions

1 In a 16-ounce (480 ml) spray bottle, combine the vinegar and alcohol.

2 If using essential oil, in a small glass bowl, stir together the essential oil and arrowroot, adding more oil by the drop until you like how it smells. Add this (or just the arrowroot if not using essential oil) to the bottle.

3 Fill the bottle with filtered water. Cover. Shake. Spray. Wipe.

Oven Cleaner

If it's the inside of your oven that needs attention, in a small glass container, combine ½ cup (110 g) baking soda and 10 to 20 drops lemon essential oil (optional). Stir in enough water to form a thick paste. Use a rag, sponge, or your hand to apply the paste over all inner surfaces of a cool oven that needs to be cleaned. Let sit for 30 minutes, or up to overnight. Wipe down with a wet cloth. The end.

Tub, Tile, Grout, Sink, and Toilet Cleaner

As good as, if not better (because you made it yourself) than those other cleaners you can buy in the store. It's super inexpensive to make and it cleans the designated items very well—plus you can use it to clean and polish stainless cookware. That said, if you don't want to make your own, I recommend using Bon Ami powder cleanser.

- ¾ cup (166 g) baking soda
- ¼ cup (60 ml) castile soap
- 1 tablespoon (15 ml) filtered water

Directions

1 In a glass container, stir together the baking soda, soap, and water.

2 Use immediately to clean and polish areas in the kitchen or bathroom, or use on pots, pans, plates, etc.

Carpet Freshener

Because . . . toddlers. Toddler feet. Potty learning. Spills. Mystery mess. Accumulated odors. Pets. Whatever. Sometimes the carpets need a little love. And our nostrils, too. I use some odor-eliminating and antibacterial essential oils. Here I use lavender, lemon, and tea tree essential oils for that purpose, but swap in whatever oils you prefer that have odor-eliminating and antibacterial properties. And, if you can find a mason jar cocktail shaker lid to use as a cover, it's perfect for this job.

- Baking soda
- Lavender essential oil
- Lemon essential oil
- Tea tree essential oil

Directions

1 Fill a mason jar or any repurposed used jar (use the Label Remover, see below, to get rid of the label) with baking soda.

2 Add 30 drops each of lavender, lemon, and tea tree essential oil (or adjust the amounts and ratios to fit what you like). Cover the jar and give it a good shake.

3 To use: Sprinkle some baking soda on the carpet or rug that needs to be refreshed and let it sit for at least 30 minutes, or up to a full day. Vacuum the carpet well and enjoy the freshness. You're welcome.

Label Remover

This concoction is great to whip up to get stickers, labels, and goo off items. It works great at removing price tags from new items, labels off jars you'd like to repurpose, stickers off water bottles, and more.

- Baking soda
- Olive oil or other cooking oil
- Few drops lemon essential oil

Directions

1 In a glass bowl, combine equal parts baking soda and olive oil (amounts used will depend on how many labels you need to remove, or their size).

2 Add the lemon essential oil and stir to combine.

3 Spread the paste over the pesky stickers and labels you want to remove. Let sit for 30 minutes or longer, then peel or scrub off the labels with ease. And without toxins.

Cleaning Tips

Set a simple, manageable weekly schedule. Do all the dusting one day, bathrooms one day, vacuuming and mopping one day, changing the bedding one day. If you have even three or four days a week where you take ten to twenty minutes to tackle that day's tasks and repeat this weekly, it's very sustainable and manageable. If it's a set day (I have Thirsty Thursdays to remind me to water the plants on time every week), this can be really helpful in maintaining a clean home without it becoming a larger, harder-to-manage task.

In addition to those weekly tasks, I have some I tend to daily. I try (and struggle) to wash, fold, and put away a load of laundry daily so the laundry doesn't become overwhelming. The more I stick to that, the less daunting laundry is for me. I clean as I go in the kitchen and keep that space tidied and clean throughout the day, so there is no set "clean the kitchen" day. Counters are tidied and cleaned daily. Floors are tidied throughout the day and definitely before bedtime. I like to wake each day to a fresh start and return to a peaceful place when I get home from being out for any amount of time. I make my bed every morning and it sets the tone for me for the day and always provides me with a calm and refreshing environment no matter what else happens in my day. Deep cleaning items like baseboards

can be scheduled, too, but much less frequently than these regular weekly tasks (see 29 for more on this).

Dust and vacuum (with a HEPA filter) regularly, which, in my opinion, is at least once a week. Microfiber cloths trap the dust particles well so you're not putting it right back into the air. An old pillowcase makes a great tool for dusting ceiling fan blades as the dust can be trapped inside as you insert each blade into the pillowcase before wiping it down.

My favorite tool for floors is a steam mop. I add lemon essential oil to the microfiber mop pad before putting it on my steam mop to add a lovely scent and boost the cleaning power. Steam is a great cleaner as it breaks up dirt and muck and can also attack unwanted visitors like harmful bacteria, mold, and viruses. No chemicals needed!

If you utilize a dishwasher, make sure to look inside for a filter. Most models have a filter that is removed easily for cleaning and that task should be done regularly. I suggest at least a few times a month. Maybe add this to your weekly schedule? I also suggest taking out any other pieces that are designed to be removed for cleaning at the same time. Leaving the dishwasher ajar or open as much as possible can help prevent mold as it will be better able to dry thoroughly and invite in light that can help keep mold at bay as well.

White vinegar can make a good rinse aid for machines that have a dispenser for that.

A note on cleaning versus disinfecting or sanitizing: Cleaning can remove dirt, germs, and muck from surfaces. Disinfecting or sanitizing kills organisms on surfaces. Many of those organisms are out there doing good work. Disinfectants and sanitizers don't play many favorites and will take out the good with the potentially bad. Most times, cleaning is the best bet.

I personally avoid disinfecting unless I think it is truly necessary, which is

rarely. Our homes have a microbiome, and when it's healthy and in balance that is a good thing. Killing off good bacteria regularly can disrupt the balance. When I feel it's worth the potential disruption, I typically opt for milder disinfectants like peroxide or alcohol. For example, I spray down my toilet brush with peroxide after cleaning the toilet and allow it to rest between the seat and toilet bowl to air-dry before storing. I also have a nifty little device that turns vinegar, salt, and water into hypochlorous acid, which disinfects like bleach without all the associated toxins.

the Bathroom

The place we go to clean ourselves is, ironically, the place we typically have the highest rate of toxin exposure in the home.

Our skin is the largest organ of our bodies and is capable of absorbing what it comes in contact with. Many ingredients in the products we apply to our bodies can be harming our health, and when we layer them on or even just add them all up in a day, it can present a problem. A typical person will easily use at least fifteen different products in a day that they have in their bathrooms. (Most of us will use more than fifteen, especially women.) Each product may contain upwards of a dozen or so individual ingredients. A little bit of this and a little bit of that adds up fast with personal care products. Most conventional personal care products contain multiple ingredients that aren't really serving our bodies or contributing to our health. Now, consider the impact of using this many products day after day after day.

Fear not! Improving this room does not need to be overwhelming or break the bank. In this chapter, I include ways to minimize, some simple swaps, a variety of DIY recipes, water toxin mitigation techniques, and more.

Note: While this is a long and detailed chapter, you can also visit the Resources section at the back of this book for product recommendations or visit alittlelesstoxic.com/resources for free product guides.

The Big Picture

Items you use daily, or with regularity, are important to consider when making your home a healthier place because of the amount of exposure you have to them. Exposure doesn't just occur while you're actively using the products, although that is obviously of greater impact. Having these products in your home at all contributes to poorer air quality and can affect the overall health of your home and those who live in it. Secondly, since these products are used regularly and need to be replaced more frequently than many other items, you have an opportunity to make simple swaps, one or two at a time, and as needed, that will add up quickly.

Recent studies show that within even three days of switching to healthier personal care products, hormone disrupting chemicals in the body, such as parabens, phthalates, and triclosan, decrease by up to 44 percent! Yes, just by switching personal care products—and in only three days.

While the bathroom can seem overwhelming due to the sheer number of products, fear not! Just use the ALLT approach (see page 9).

Bathroom Inventory

An average bathroom includes so many things we put in, on, and around our bodies:

- Air freshener
- Bath bubbles
- Body wash and/or body soap
- Cotton swabs and rounds
- Deodorant
- Feminine hygiene products
- Hair spray, gel, mousse, and other hair products
- Hand soap
- Lotion and moisturizer
- Makeup (typically more than ten items, often more): blush, bronzer, concealer, eyebrow pencil, eyeliner, eyeshadows, foundation, lip balm and lipsticks, mascara, powder, etc.
- Mesh sponge, washcloth, etc.
- Nail polish and remover
- Over-the-counter treatments and medications
- Perfume and/or cologne
- Serums and creams
- Shampoo and conditioner
- Shave cream, razor, and aftershave
- Shower curtain and rugs
- Toilet paper, toothpaste, floss, and mouthwash
- Towels
- Wipes

Bath and Shower Water

As I discussed in the Kitchen chapter (see page 45), municipal water comes into your home free of bacteria because of the use of some materials that can be pretty toxic. Some of these things aren't the best for our hair and skin, and can be drying and irritating, causing harm to the protective skin barrier and microbiome. These sanitizing treatments can be indiscriminate and kill beneficial microbes on your body. Ingredients like chloramine and chlorine are even more toxic when in hot water as they become gases that travel in vapors to our lungs. Showering and bathing in chlorinated tap water can increase toxic exposure because you have the exposure through absorption in your skin as well as inhalation of the more toxic vapors. If you don't have a whole-house filter, there are some simple, low-cost ways to minimize toxic exposures in our shower and bath water.

A shower filter that reduces or eliminates chloramine and chlorine can be purchased and added between the pipe and the showerhead very easily and without a professional plumber. The filter, typically, needs to be replaced about once a year. There are several options for bath water, too. You can fill your tub with the now-filtered showerhead or use items like bath filters that typically hang

over the bath spigot, or float in the tub, and that filter the water before it enters the tub. Many of these types of filters use ascorbic acid (synthetic vitamin C) internally as ascorbic acid can neutralize chlorine rapidly. My cheap fix for the bath is to add about a teaspoon of ascorbic acid powder to the tub while it's filling to neutralize chlorine. I keep a bottle of ascorbic acid in the bathroom because I'm much more likely to remember to use something and actually do it when I can see it and it's within reach.

Cotton Products

There are quite a few places fibers, like cotton, appear in the bathroom. Choosing healthy fibers is beneficial. Opting for organic cotton, when possible, can help, too.

Here are some typical items in the bathroom made with cotton or other fabric:

- Bath mat and rugs
- Cotton balls or rounds
- Cotton swabs
- Hand towels, bath towels, and washcloths
- Shower curtain
- Tampons, liners, and pads
- Toilet paper

Natural fibers are superior to synthetic for a healthier home for a number of reasons (see page 138 for more on this), including the fact that synthetics are typically chemically treated and/or are byproducts of petroleum, making them, essentially, plastic. In the bathroom, those plastic and chemically treated fibers may pose more of a threat because of the typically hot and steamy room that is commonly sealed off daily.

Shower Curtains

For shower curtains, I love a natural fiber curtain, but I also want to keep my walls and floors from becoming wet, especially with mold being a common uninvited guest in the bathroom (more on that in a bit). Hemp is a little more mold resistant than cotton whereas cotton is slightly more water resistant than hemp. For a little more water resistance that's still pretty low tox, nylon can be a good choice. For the best water and mildew resistance that's not quite as healthy as the natural fibers but still A Little Less Toxic than the PVC and other plastic options, PEVA (sometimes called EVA) may be a good fit for your shower. In my home currently we use a PEVA liner under a cotton curtain and wash both regularly.

Bath Mat

There are some great, healthier, options for bath mats, including wood and stone, and increasingly retailers are carrying natural fiber and organic natural fiber options. Like other rugs, I prefer one without any backing glued on as the glues are not healthy for the air in the home and, again, we're talking about using this in a room that is regularly hot and steamy. If slipping is a concern, a silicone or rubber pad can be used under any bath mat you choose. I love the no-backing mat here, too, because I can throw it in the wash.

Towels and Washcloths

These items, more commonly, are cotton or a cotton blend that includes synthetic fibers such as polyester. Polyester is a byproduct of petroleum (more on this in the Bedroom chapter, see page 138). When your towels need to be replaced, choose new items with 100 percent natural fibers (and preferably organic) for a healthier option. Towels can be expensive, so this might be an item that gets replaced later or more slowly.

Cotton Hygiene Products

When it comes to balls, liners, pads, rounds, swabs, and tampons, these items are used on our bodies and in some pretty tender areas. Cotton is the most highly sprayed crop in the world since it is not used for consumption. More than 95 percent of cotton crops are nonorganic and are then covered in toxic pesticides. Cotton, alone, uses nearly half of the world's agrochemical pesticides while only accounting for 2 to 3 percent of the world's crops. And seven of the fifteen pesticides used on cotton are listed as "probable," "likely," or "known" carcinogens by the Environmental Protection Agency. Heavy pesticide treatment becomes part of the plant and doesn't merely wash out. To prepare conventional cotton for use in fabrics and other products, like cotton rounds, swabs, tampons, etc., the cotton is heavily treated with chlorine, fragrances, formaldehyde, silicone waxes, softeners, and other toxins.

My method is not to panic and throw out all my cotton products. Rather, when I run out of cotton swabs or tampons or other cotton products, I look for a better replacement. Try organic cotton for these items. The price isn't much more and the positive difference it makes is well worth it. Organic cotton products are free of synthetic and toxic pesticides and typically are free of chlorine, fragrance, and other known toxins.

Feminine Hygiene Products

For feminine hygiene products specifically, switching to organic or other less-toxic options can have an immediate and measurable result. Many women report a noticeable improvement in their physical and/or menstrual health within a cycle or two. Vaginal and vulvar tissues are highly permeable and sensitive. Conventional sanitary pads may contain plastic made from crude oil in amounts as much as the equivalent of four plastic grocery bags. Most women who use these products go through a couple dozen or more a month. That's a lot of plastic against a vulnerable body part. Conventional pads and tampons are also made with pesticide-laden cotton. They also typically contain odor neutralizers and fragrance, which contain phthalates as well as other

chemicals such as VOCs, PEG, PET, dyes, bleach, and adhesives. Many of these components can disrupt healthy hormone function as well as contribute to other health issues. Dioxins, for example, are commonly found in the materials used to bleach feminine hygiene products. Dioxins are being researched as a plausible link to cancer.

Healthier options include organic cotton items such as pads and tampons. Being certified organic can help ensure they are free of synthetic pesticides, fragrance, dyes, chlorine bleach, and other unwanted toxins. As always, read the ingredients and never be scared to ask questions. Medical-grade silicone menstrual cups can be a great option for many. One cup can last years and be great for the budget and environment as well as being a low-tox option that many find easier to use and more freeing than cotton options, once you get the hang of it. They typically hold about as much as three tampons in fluid and so only need to be emptied two to four times a day, making them less fuss than tampons or pads. Also, washable and reusable cotton pad options are making a big comeback. Much like how cloth diapers have advanced, these types of cotton pads have come a long way! Look out for any using plastic or treated with stain-resistant chemicals.

Toilet Paper

I realize this topic can be a hot-button issue in some homes, where people are very committed to a certain ply or brand. Then, there's the whole over vs. under debate. I'll settle that for you. The roll should spin over! Beards are better than mullets.

There are levels of TP. On the most basic level, toilet paper is made from paper. Conventional TP is bleached. That's already problematic. This stuff is rubbing some tender spaces. The "ultra-strong" type of TP is typically bleached as well as treated with *formaldehyde*. The kind with lotion or that carries other marketing like "extra soft" is bleached and can include petroleum-based oil and "fragrance," which can contain dozens to hundreds of chemicals that don't have to be disclosed (see page 15 for more on fragrance). Recycled TP is made with previously bleached papers, sometimes bleached again, and often uses recycled thermal paper, which is notorious for its high levels of BPA (see page 16 for more on why BPA is a problem). Bleach, BPA, formaldehyde, fragrance, and petrochemicals have no business being up in your business. These things can contribute to many health concerns, including cancers, hormone disruption, infertility, inflammation, libido problems, neurological disorders, and more.

Healthier alternatives are more readily available as we, the informed consumers, are looking for better options for ourselves and our families. Yet cotton varieties that are unbleached, without fragrance, formaldehyde, or BPA, are still hard to find. To get a low-tox TP, avoid any with claims like extra strong or ultra-soft or any signs it contains "lotion." Look for unbleached TP and avoid recycled items unless the maker provides testing to ensure the end product is free of BPA, BPF, and BPS. Currently, the best TP options are made using bamboo. No bleach, formaldehyde, fragrance, or petrochemicals—yet very soft and durable.

Another excellent option is a bidet—a stand-alone fixture or a simple fixture that attaches to your toilet and that you use to spray your bits with water, typically temperature controlled, to clean yourself after using the potty. This "eliminates" the need for toilet paper research and shopping. Modern bidets attach easily and work well. They come in a large range of prices, but there are plenty that are affordable. Many people who have tried them have become bidet converts, finding them more sanitary than toilet paper, reporting better hygiene and comfort. They can be better environmentally and economically than TP, too.

Personal Care Products

I can't possibly go over every single product or even category and talk about potential problems and alternatives regarding personal care products. Nor would anyone want to read all of that! Instead, I can talk about some potentially harmful and unnecessary ingredients and how we can mitigate or avoid them while still having wonderful and effective products, all without breaking the bank.

As I mentioned, dozens upon dozens of personal care products live in a typical bathroom. Many of them contain the same problematic ingredients, so while, for example, phthalates may not be much to fret over for occasional use (although many would argue they're not safe in any amount), most people layer on phthalate after phthalate through a variety of products and throughout the day. Most conventional personal care and toiletry products contain several of these concerning ingredients in some combination.

Let's look at some of the most common offenders and some that can pose a bigger threat even in lesser amounts:

- Artificial dyes
- BHA and BHT
- Bisphenols
- Formaldehyde
- Fragrance/parfum
- Heavy metals, including lead and aluminum
- Parabens
- PEGs (polyethylene glycols and polysorbates)
- Petroleum
- PFAS
- Phthalates
- Retinyl palmitate a.k.a. retinoic acid or vitamin A
- SLS (sodium laureth sulfate)
- Triclosan

Hair Care

Healthy hair begins with a healthy scalp. Then, go one step further: The scalp is skin and skin health begins with a healthy gut. That means magical hair products can only do so much! Most hair care products are highly engineered, contain many chemicals, and are highly fragranced. This means that the chemicals stay on your head and hair and you breathe them in all day, every day. In addition to this, these concoctions, while creating temporary shine, can be clogging to hair follicles as well as damaging to the hair and scalp, leading to weaker, duller, more damaged hair over time. One of the simplest ways to begin swapping out hair care products as you go is to find a replacement that has no use of the word "fragrance" in the ingredients. This will narrow your search in a major way. Chances are, if there is no "fragrance," most of the other top ingredients I avoid are absent as well. I have found quite a few brands for "healthier" hair care for all different uses and types and textures of hair, and many are comparable in price to the conventional stuff.

Apple Cider Vinegar Rinse

Skin has a pH level that is slightly acidic, around 5.5 on the pH scale for most people. This slightly acidic level is protective and helps fend off fungi, irritants, pollutants, toxicants, and damaging bacteria. Shampoo is usually around pH level 8, much more alkaline than our skin likes to be. Water is also slightly more alkaline than our skin. When we wet and shampoo our hair, we temporarily alter the healthy acidic pH level, which can disrupt the balance and health of our scalp and hair. This will self-correct over time, but the faster we can bring our pH back into balance, the healthier our scalp and hair will be. Although some shampoos claim to be pH balanced, this is typically achieved with more chemicals and I prefer to avoid that. Instead, I use a simple spray of apple cider vinegar diluted with water after every wash.

This apple cider vinegar rinse can balance the scalp's pH; seal the hair cuticle, making it stronger, smoother, and shinier; help prevent breakage; combat fungi and bacteria; treat dandruff; soothe an irritated and itchy scalp; tame frizz; and potentially promote hair growth. This batch size lasts my family of four a few weeks, but of course, feel free to scale it up or down.

- 2 tablespoons (30 ml) apple cider vinegar (ACV)
- 1 cup (240 ml) filtered water

Directions

In a 12- to 16-ounce (360 to 480 ml) spray bottle, combine the vinegar and filtered water. Cover and shake gently to combine.

To use, spritz your scalp and roots after shampooing and conditioning. Let the rinse run down through your hair and do not rinse it out. Vinegar absorbs odor and then dissipates, so you will not smell like vinegar. (Also, it's diluted.)

If you prefer, you can mix up a batch in a measuring cup and pour it over your head at the end of your wash and condition routine. It is safe for all hair types. Just be careful not to get it in your eyes.

Hair Clarifying Treatment

Over time, the scalp and hair can accumulate buildup of matter including dead skin cells, product, sebum, and other things. This can contribute to dull and lifeless hair. It can also contribute to hair breakage, dandruff, fungi, itchy and flaky scalp, and more. Clarifying breaks down and removes this unwanted stuff.

Clarifying will open the hair cuticle, which can lead to further damage, so it's not recommended to use clarifying treatments regularly. I do this treatment a few times a year as I feel it's needed. I'd probably not do it more than once per month. Opening the cuticle may allow for dye pigment to be lifted so it may not be great to do after a fresh coloring. Baking soda can be irritating to some skin so maybe sample a swatch first and avoid the scalp if necessary.

- ½ cup (110 g) baking soda
- 1½ cups (360 ml) filtered water

Directions

In a small bowl, stir together the baking soda and filtered water until the baking soda dissolves.

Gently massage the clarifying treatment into the scalp and hair, root to tips. Leave on for 1 to 3 minutes. Rinse with warm water.

I like to follow this treatment with Apple Cider Vinegar Rinse (see page 90). The baking soda opens the cuticle to release buildup, plus it's quite alkaline. The vinegar in the rinse will rebalance the scalp pH and reseal that clean hair cuticle. Pour it all down the hair, starting at the scalp. You can rinse it off, but I don't. No other shampoo or conditioner is needed on clarifying day. This takes the place of my regular wash and condition and I carry on as usual until the next wash.

Oral Hygiene

A healthy body requires a healthy gut. A healthy gut can't exist without a healthy oral microbiome. Your mouth is the entryway to your gut and where the approximately thirty feet of the tubing running through your entire body begins. That long tube is your GI tract, and it plays critical roles in your immune health and overall wellness.

The mouth houses around seven hundred kinds of organisms creating a balance of microflora and microfauna. These organisms create the oral microbiota, one of the most complex microbial communities in the human body. Studies indicate the health of this oral microbiome plays major roles in overall health and contributes to systemic illness and disease, including autoimmune disorders, cancers, mental illnesses, pregnancy outcomes, viral infection outcomes, and more.

Some ways to repair and maintain a healthy oral microbiome include:

- Avoid the use of harsh mouthwashes.

- Brush regularly with good toothpaste.

- Drink plenty of water.

- Eat a diet rich in whole, mineral-rich foods, including lots of veggies, healthy fats, and proteins.

- Floss regularly with floss that doesn't contain toxic ingredients like PFAS.

- Maintain regular dental cleanings, preferably by dentists who are current on studies involving the importance of the oral microbiome, including holistic dentists.

- Mouth taping (see page 144)

- Reduce phytic acid intake by properly preparing grains.

- Try tongue scraping and oil pulling (see below).

Tongue Scraping and Oil Pulling

Scraping the surface of the tongue from back to front using a material like a stainless-steel or copper device designed for this or even the edge of a spoon can have many health benefits. Tongue scraping can help remove plaque and bacteria from the tongue much better than a brush can. It can also improve your sense of taste, breath odor, and overall health.

Oil pulling is the act of swishing about 1 tablespoon (15 ml) of a specific edible oil or blend of oils in the mouth for between 5 and 20 minutes. Coconut and sesame oils are my favorites. I keep a container of coconut oil in my bathroom for this. Do not spit oil into the sink drain as it can clog the pipes. The trash can or garden is a better disposal area. Oil pulling is believed to help pull toxins from the body as well as whiten teeth, reduce harmful bacteria in the mouth, reduce bad breath and cavities, and even, potentially, reduce inflammation in the body.

Toothpaste

This was a very difficult item for me to replace with conventional options. Any toothpaste I found without fluoride had other ingredients I didn't love or seemed to be missing ingredients I thought were important. So, I began making my own DIY Toothpaste (page 97). Unlike DIY laundry soap, which never quite got me to the performance level of commercial detergents, I can say that, with my homemade toothpaste, I've never had my mouth feel as clean. I have had no dental issues in the years I exclusively used homemade toothpaste. Still, in recent years, some wonderful commercial options have become available for purchase.

Here are some ingredients in most toothpaste that I avoid:

Artificial flavors: These can contain dozens or more chemicals that don't have to be disclosed and may contribute to health issues.

Blue #1 or other dyes: Carcinogens and neurotoxins linked to behavioral disorders and learning problems.

Fluoride: A known neurotoxin, found in high amounts in the brains of victims of Alzheimer's, that also aids the absorption of aluminum. More recent research on this byproduct of some metal manufacturing is showing less benefit to teeth than previously believed; it's also revealing the many associated side effects. I choose not to have this ingredient absorbed through the delicate tissues in my mouth.

Propylene glycol: Added for texture; it is also the main ingredient in most antifreeze.

Sodium laureth sulfate (SLS): This ingredient makes toothpaste foam. Foam doesn't clean, but we're conditioned to believe bubbles do. They don't. SLS is a skin irritant and implicated in oral problems, including canker sores.

Triclosan: Antimicrobial, meaning it can harm or kill beneficial microbes. Also, a suspected carcinogen and a known hormone disruptor.

On the other hand, here are some ingredients I love:

Bentonite clay: This clay from the Earth is naturally rich in minerals, including calcium, magnesium, and silica, and are good for teeth. It also has antibacterial properties and detoxifying abilities. It may also help remineralize teeth as well as clean and protect them.

Hydroxyapatite: Move over, fluoride! This mineral, a form of calcium, is a major component of your bones and teeth: 97 percent of tooth enamel and 70 percent of dentin are made of hydroxyapatite. HA has been scientifically proven to strengthen and protect teeth without fluoride. It can chemically bind to teeth to fill and shield them while rebuilding and strengthening teeth as well

as protecting them. It also helps whiten teeth naturally. Although hydroxyapatite is not as well known in the United States, it's been the gold standard in Japan for more than forty years. It's nontoxic and safe enough to eat, though you probably shouldn't. In fact, it's so safe and beneficial, the recommendation is to not rinse after brushing with toothpaste containing hydroxyapatite. Some seriously amazing stuff.

Salt or trace mineral drops: Good salt contains many trace minerals that can benefit teeth. It can also work as a gentle abrasive for cleaning teeth. Trace minerals are a great alternative.

DIY Toothpaste

In this recipe, you have everything you need. The calcium bentonite clay polishes, brightens, and remineralizes. The baking soda helps clean and brighten, and salt adds a bit of remineralizing power as well. The coconut oil is antimicrobial and generally healing. It may help reduce plaque and lower inflammation. And of course, some essential oils for their potential benefits as well as flavor!

- 3 tablespoons (35 g) calcium bentonite clay
- 1 teaspoon baking soda
- 10 to 20 drops trace minerals, or a pinch of good salt
- 2 tablespoons (30 ml) liquid or fractionated coconut oil
- 1 or 2 drops food-grade essential oil (I like a drop or two of any combination of cinnamon, peppermint, and vanilla; optional)
- Filtered water

Do not use metal to measure, mix, or store this toothpaste.

Directions

In a glass container, using a wooden spoon, stir together the clay, baking soda, trace minerals, coconut oil, and essential oil (if using). Stir in 1 to 3 teaspoons (up to 15 ml) of water to reach your desired consistency. Store in a glass jar with a tight-fitting lid, or a silicone squeeze tube.

Tooth Whitening

Following the previously mentioned tips regarding toothpaste will be very helpful in maintaining brighter, whiter teeth. I'm no stranger to tea or an occasional glass of red wine, plus I've got some large chompers and laughing is one of my favorite pastimes, so I like to use a little more support to keep mine nice and white. But I do so without the use of chemicals. I used to be a big fan of the big brand store-bought whitening strips, and would use them occasionally, even though they left me aching for days, and sometimes weeks, with sensitivity. I switched over to charcoal powder years ago and love it!

Charcoal powder brightens and whitens with the first use, and with regular use or maintenance, it can be just as effective as the whitening strips, but without the toxins or the sensitivity. Plus, it's super cost-effective. Some people use additional ingredients like bentonite and baking soda, and food-grade lemon or orange essential oil for added effectiveness. I have also found some whitening strips that work fantastically while using great ingredients and are safe for my oral microbiome. They don't cause me any sensitivity or discomfort either.

Skin Care

Your skin is your body's largest organ. It is capable of absorbing what it comes in contact with and what is put on it. It is also designed with a brilliant protective barrier and defense system. Overcleansing, using harsh, antibacterial, or irritating ingredients on our skin, can damage our natural defenses, the health of our skin, and our bodies.

Your skin has a unique microbiome. The makeup of the microscopic organisms that reside on your skin is as unique as your fingertip—and it has great purpose. When healthy and balanced, this community of invisible guests acts almost as its own organ and affects your entire body, including mood, immune function, aging, and more. Protecting the healthy balance of microbes on your skin makes a big difference not only to your skin but also to the rest of you.

The skin microbiome also houses what is known as the acid mantle. A healthy acid mantle has a balanced microbiome and helps protect the skin by repelling toxins, irritants, and contaminants. When our skin microbiome or acid mantle becomes compromised, we become compromised. What we use on our skin matters.

A note on antibacterial soaps and hand sanitizers: Killing 99.9 percent of bacteria on our skin may seem like a good thing when we fear a few organisms. There are very many more organisms that reside in, on, and around us that offer myriad health benefits and work to aid and protect us. Killing 99.9 percent means the only 0.1 percent that survives are the most resistant and/or the strongest. The strongest will be the ones left to repopulate, thereby altering the balance of microbes. The strongest become more proliferating, invasive, and problematic. Thus, they are harder to balance or eliminate. Superbugs are real and I've been a victim of them. The topic needs to be taken seriously.

Keep in mind the difference between cleaning and sanitizing. *Cleaning* our skin removes dirt and impurities. It's necessary sometimes, but probably not as often as we've been conditioned to believe. I'm all for regular hand washing and being cleanly. I do not, however, want a sterile environment. The frequency of cleaning and what we use to clean our skin matter. Some soaps strip oils, alter the pH, and deplete the microbiome that are all there for our health and the health of our skin. *Sanitizing* our skin does not discriminate between beneficial microbes and the few that may pose a problem. Clean is superior to sanitized. Even with hands. I refrain from sanitizing anything outside of true need, especially my skin.

One way I have improved the health of my skin, eliminated several personal care products, and simplified my life is with *jojoba oil*. This lovely oil is made from the seed of the jojoba plant. It is highly stable and doesn't go rancid quickly or easily.

Here are some other of jojoba oil's features and benefits:

- Antibacterial, antifungal, hypoallergenic, nontoxic, great for all skin types

- A polyunsaturated wax, making it a great skin protector

- Contains vitamins and minerals, including B complex, E, chromium, copper, iodine, silicon, and zinc, making jojoba oil highly therapeutic

- Highly emollient: soothes and moisturizes the skin

- High in antioxidants

- Removes makeup easily and effectively and is an overall effective skin cleanser

- Similar to skin's natural sebum in structure, it removes excess yuck, balances oils, and moisturizes well, without clogging pores (noncomedogenic) or remaining oily or sticky on the skin

I use jojoba as a face and body moisturizer. It works best when applied to damp skin as it spreads nicely and will trap the moisture underneath to help keep the skin hydrated. I have made many wonderful homemade serums with jojoba as the base. I also use it to cleanse my face in the evenings, with nothing else, and find it to be the best face cleanser I've ever used. It removes dirt and impurities without stripping my skin of beneficial oils, even removing heavy or waterproof makeup easily and without damaging my skin or lashes.

How to Oil Cleanse

I know it sounds counterintuitive to clean with oil. I also know that this might scare you if you have oily or acne-prone skin. I was one of those people whom this would freak out. Oily, combo skin, acne, and afraid of pore clogging. Hear me out. Like dissolves like. Cleansing with oil makes so much sense. It melts away makeup, dirt, and impurities with ease without clogging your pores and without irritating your skin. It will not make you more oily.

Overproduction of oil commonly occurs when the skin is repeatedly dried out. Bringing the skin back into better balance can't happen by drying it out. Oil stripping is the last thing you want to do as that will only make matters worse. Oil cleansing is good for virtually all skin types and concerns. In light of everything we just talked about with the microbiome and acid mantle, skin-friendly oil is where it's at!

I pump some plain organic cold-pressed jojoba in my hand. I rub it all over my face until everything is dissolved and looks like it's melting away, then gently wipe it all off with a warm, wet cloth. Some people follow up with another face cleanser for what is called double cleansing, but I find it unnecessary (but you do what works for you!). Follow up with any additional skin care, if you fancy. Face washing no longer leaves makeup behind, burns my eyes, gets water all over me and the bathroom, or dries out or irritates my skin. Without altering my pH balance with cleansers, I no longer have the need to "tone" my skin after cleansing so I've eliminated that step as well. Simpler, better, cheaper.

What about the Body?

When washing skin that's not on my face, I still look for gentle cleansers that include nontoxic cleansing ingredients. They may include fats like olive or coconut oil or shea butter, goat's milk, and prebiotics, like in one favorite that contains sea kelp.

For lotions and body balms, when I want more than my trusty jojoba, I love blends that contain things like almond oil, aloe vera, beeswax, shea butter, or tallow from pastured cows. Again, the main thing when choosing is to read ingredient labels, ignore marketing claims on the packaging, and avoid things like "fragrance."

Foaming Hand Soap

You can easily stretch the soap you buy to make it last longer, or make your own hand soap with ingredients you love. Reuse an old foaming soap bottle or purchase a new one. If using castile soap, I recommend saving a little room for some almond oil and/or aloe as castile is very drying.

- Filtered water
- Castile soap or your favorite liquid hand or body soap

Directions

Fill your foaming soap container three-fourths full of filtered water. Then, fill it the rest of the way with castile soap. Mix and use.

Body Cleanse

This recipe is for a 16-ounce (480 ml) container, though you can easily adjust the measurements for any size or type of container. Other favorite containers for this are a travel silicone goo tube or a glass pump bottle. I loved this cleanser when the babies were in diapers to spray on a clean cloth to use as a cleansing wipe. They're a bit older now but we still use it for a quick cleaning of a berry-stained face or feet that have been exploring in the garden. We always bring this cleanser with us when camping, too, to clean up while living outdoors without a sink or shower. It comes in handy quite a bit.

- 1 tablespoon (15 ml) witch hazel
- 1 tablespoon (15 ml) skin-soothing oil (such as almond, my favorite, or jojoba)
- 1 tablespoon (15 ml) aloe
- 2 tablespoons (30 ml) liquid body wash or hand soap
- 2 drops lavender essential oil (optional)
- 2 drops tea tree essential oil (optional)
- Filtered water

Directions

In a 16-ounce (480 ml) container with a lid, combine the witch hazel, oil, aloe, soap, and essential oils (if using). Fill the container with filtered water. Cover, shake, and use.

the bathroom

DIY Foaming Makeup Brush and Sponge Cleanser

I love this blend for cleaning my makeup brushes and sponges and have been using it for years. It's simple to mix up and incredibly inexpensive. One bottle lasts me many months. Plus, it works well and is, as always, A Little Less Toxic.

- Filtered water
- ¼ cup (60 ml) castile soap (I like lavender, but any will do)
- 1 tablespoon (15 ml) oil of choice (I like fractionated coconut oil for this, but jojoba, olive, almond, and others are great, too)
- Tea tree essential oil

Directions

Using any foaming pump dispenser, pour in the filtered water first, to about two-thirds of the way to the max fill line. Adding the water first helps prevent excess bubbles from forming.

In a small dish, stir together the soap, oil, and a few drops of essential oil. Pour the soap mixture into the bottle. Close. Shake. Use.

Note: Pure castile soap is a great cleanser. It's made of saponified organic oils and essential oils for the scent and cleansing properties. I do not like this type of soap for skin because of its high pH and its propensity to dry out skin and damage the acid mantle, but it's great for cleaning all manner of other things around the house.

The oil will extend the life of your foam pump but it's also useful for conditioning the delicate hairs and fibers of your makeup brushes. I choose fractionated coconut oil for this: "Fractionated" means it will remain in a liquid state even at cooler temperatures. Don't use regular coconut oil for this as it can solidify and clog the pump. Coconut oil is known to help combat acne, and is conditioning, antifungal, and antibacterial.

Tea tree essential oil is known for its antifungal and antiseptic properties, among many things. A few drops will help eliminate yuck from your tools that can clog pores, contribute to eczema, acne, aging, and other skin issues.

2-Ingredient Detox Mask

This detox mask can help draw out toxins, gently exfoliate skin, reduce the appearance of scars, unclog pores, and help even skin tone. I like to use this on occasion and not more than once a week.

Do not use metal to measure, mix, or store this mask as it can deactivate the clay.

- Bentonite clay
- Filtered water or apple cider vinegar

Directions

In a glass bowl, using a wooden spoon, stir together equal parts clay and filtered water or vinegar.

Spread the mask over your face in a nice ⅛- to ¼-inch (0.3 to 0.6 cm) layer (neck and décolletage area, too, if you like), avoiding the eyes. Let dry. Leave it on for at least 5 minutes and up to 45 minutes.

Rinse well with warm water. Pat dry and follow up with a gentle moisturizer.

Honey Mask

This is one of the simplest DIY self-care items you can make: one simple ingredient—honey. Honey can help balance the bacteria on your skin to help treat acne. Honey is also soothing and healing for the skin and can help treat skin issues topically such as psoriasis and eczema. Honey can also increase skin moisture, clean pores, gently exfoliate, lighten scars, reduce fine lines and wrinkles, and brighten complexion. A honey mask can be applied multiple times a week, if desired. You can add more ingredients, like fresh lemon juice, ground turmeric (beware, it can stain skin and clothing), and/or yogurt, for extra benefits. Get creative but be mindful of the delicate balance of your skin.

- Raw or manuka honey

Directions

Apply a thin layer of honey to your face, avoiding the eyes. Leave on for about 15 minutes or so. You can tap the honey with the pads of your fingers and pull away to help encourage lymph flow.

Rinse with warm water. Pat dry and moisturize as usual.

Detox Baths

Our bodies are designed to detox regularly. We come into contact with toxic offenders every day—even when we live a life being intentional about reducing toxic exposures. Through air, skin contact, ingestion, injection, and proximity exposure, our bodies can take on a toxic burden that can lead to a host of issues ranging from skin irritation to chronic disease and anything in between. While we look for ways to reduce our toxin exposure, we can take steps to help our bodies remove and eliminate what the body sees as offenders. One way is a detox bath.

A detox bath is just a long soak, which is useful to allow time for the toxins to be pulled out: 40 minutes or more is ideal. Rinse with cool water and make sure to drink plenty of water afterward. Do this a couple times a week or more, as your schedule allows.

Here are some ideas for things to add to your bath:

Apple cider vinegar: Vinegar made of fermented apple juice; helps draw toxins out through the skin. It also helps balance skin pH and is anti-inflammatory. ACV can help soothe many skin ailments, including bug bites, dry skin, eczema, sunburn, yeast, and more. And, some say it even helps with joint pain. Add 1 cup (240 ml) or so to an adult bath or ½ cup (120 ml) to a child's bath.

Calcium bentonite clay: Volcanic ash; functions like a magnet. Bonds to metals to help draw heavy metals, including aluminum, cadmium, lead, and mercury that can enter the body through myriad pathways, and helps draw them out. Avoid contact with metal when adding this to your bath. Use ¼ to ½ cup (46 to 92 g) in a full bath, or 2 tablespoons up to ¼ cup (23 to 46 g) for a child's bath.

Epsom salts: Magnesium sulfate; a potent mineral compound. Creates a type of reverse osmosis effect in the water that helps pull toxins from the body. It can also help draw out infection. Add 2 cups (499 g) to a full bath for an adult or 1 cup (250 g) for a smaller bath for children (see page 108 for more on this).

Epsom Salts Baths

Few love a good soak as much as I do. I already told you I add a teaspoon of ascorbic acid to the tub to neutralize chlorine, but I also like using Epsom salts (a.k.a. magnesium sulfate).

Magnesium sulfate soaks have been reported to:

- Assist the body in toxin elimination
- Boost internal magnesium levels
- Improve skin barrier function
- Improve sleep quality
- Lower stress levels
- Reduce muscle aches, pain, and inflammation
- Relax muscles
- Soothe achy joints and itchy and irritated skin

Magnesium sulfate can aid in the absorption of magnesium, for which most people are deficient. Some may be absorbed transdermally and, in effect, help increase the body's level of this critically important mineral. Magnesium plays a role in many of the body's important functions, including detoxing, electrical impulses, energy production, enzyme regulation, and muscle control.

Adding it to a soak has also been shown to improve skin barrier function, which can help relieve irritation, increase skin moisture, improve skin health, and reduce some symptoms of skin conditions, including psoriasis and eczema.

Sometimes, in my house we get fancy and use *magnesium flakes* (magnesium chloride), which we use more sparingly because it is more expensive, but it may increase the benefits listed previously because of its greater magnesium content and ability to be absorbed transdermally. I buy both in bulk to save a little money.

An important note: There is no one size fits all here. There are those who do not experience these benefits and some who even become ill when using compounds containing sulfur, like Epsom salts, and even magnesium chloride. Those with a CBS genetic mutation may find themselves in the group that does not tolerate Epsom soaks. If you get nauseated or experience negative effects after an Epsom soak, discontinue use.

Lymphatic System Care

Our lymphatic system is part of our circulatory and immune systems and helps remove toxins and waste from our bodies. Unlike other systems, like the circulatory system, the lymph system doesn't have a heart, or pump. It requires movement and stimulation. We can assist our bodies by encouraging lymphatic drainage through movement and exercise, sweating, self-massage, and techniques like dry brushing and gua sha.

Dry Brushing

Potential Benefits of Dry Brushing

- Claims of reduction or elimination of cellulite

- Exfoliates dry skin

- Helps detoxify the body by promoting lymph flow and drainage; many lymph systems are just below the skin

- Improves immune function

- Increases and supports blood circulation

- Is energizing

- Possibly reduces inflammation

- Potentially improves muscle tone

- Stimulates the nervous system, which can make you feel invigorated

- Unclogs pores and even reduces pore size (use a much gentler brush on your face)

Here's how to do it: Pick a natural-bristle brush with firm bristles for your body, or one with soft bristles for your face. Brush before bathing or showering. Start at the bottoms of feet and the palms of hands and brush the skin with long, gentle strokes.

Always work toward your heart, to help you remember the direction, to move things toward the lymph so it can drain out. Repeat in each area several times. Use a clockwise circular pattern on your underarms and tummy. It's best to do this in the morning or during the daytime as it can be very stimulating and keep you awake.

Gua Sha

Gua sha is an ancient beauty practice and technique that comes from traditional Chinese medicine with more than four thousand years of history. "Gua sha" literally translates to "scraping of sand" or "tiny pebbles." It helps encourage lymphatic movement and drainage, similar to dry brushing (see page 109). It also helps relieve stress and tension and can support lymphatic drainage, which is important for detoxification, and help de-puff and detoxify the skin, as well as smooth fine lines and wrinkles.

Potential Benefits of Gua Sha

- Calms the nervous system
- Can reduce stress
- Clears blockages and buildup of toxins and excess fluid
- Decreases discoloration from sun damage and acne scarring
- Increases circulation
- Promotes collagen production
- Promotes lymphatic drainage
- Reduces puffiness, including under the eyes
- Relaxes muscle tension and tightness
- Restores mobility and elasticity to tissues

Here's how to do it: Use a face-friendly oil or serum and a very smooth stone made for gua sha. Use light to medium pressure and hold the stone almost flat against your skin. Experiment with different angles of the stone, always being mindful to be gentle with your delicate skin. Repeat each stroke at least three times. Work toward the lymph areas around your face and neck. Relax and enjoy.

The Medicine Cabinet

Because I'm a believer in food as medicine, some of my "medicine cabinet" exists in the kitchen. I try to remain reasonably stocked without living in fear. I choose to be "prepared not panicked." This includes keeping frozen pineapple and other staples on hand at all times for an emergency batch of my Homemade Cough Elixir (page 112). I don't let us run too low on items that can keep us from needing medical intervention. I also keep a well-stocked first-aid kit, which you can read more about on page 112.

Okay, so with those bits out of the way, in my bathroom medicine cabinet, you're likely to find:

- Alcohol prep pads
- Contact lens solution (formaldehyde-free)
- Diphenhydramine (antihistamine)
- HOCl (hypochlorous acid) spray and gel
- Ibuprofen and acetaminophen, without dyes or artificial flavors
- Plastic-free bandages with less-toxic adhesive ingredients
- Random assortment of things my husband uses, including beard oil, razor, way too many toenail clippers, contact lens case, comb (missing teeth, I might add), and one piece of a retainer
- Thermometer
- Toothbrushes, toothpaste, charcoal, and floss
- Turmeric and ginger tincture for pain, inflammation, digestive upset

Homemade Cough Elixir

This effective cough formula has been a lifesaver for my family, and lots of others, too. In addition to sipping it, it can be frozen in small gummy molds for soothing, cooling lozenges, in ice-cube trays to be added to smoothies, or in ice pop molds for a healing treat.

- 2 cups (330 g) fresh or (280 g) frozen pineapple chunks
- Juice of 2 lemons
- 1 cup (320 g) raw organic honey
- ½ cup (120 ml) olive oil
- 1-inch (2.5 cm) piece fresh ginger
- Pinch of cayenne pepper
- Pinch of salt

Directions

In a blender, combine all the elixir ingredients. Blend well. Pour through a fine-mesh strainer set over a bowl to remove any ginger fibers for anyone sensitive to that. Transfer to an airtight container and refrigerate up to 1 week, or freeze for up to a few months. To use, take sips as often as needed.

First-Aid Kit

I have a water-resistant case that's not too heavy, but sturdy, that I keep my supplies in. Every January, I check expiration dates and refresh or replace any item that will expire before the year's end. The still-usable items that won't last until the following January enter our at-home supply of emergency goods until they are used or no longer usable. I picked January because it's easy for me to remember. New year, be ready. My goals for my kit are that it keeps us prepared and not panicked in the event of an emergency, it is comprehensive but not excessive, is portable, and is A Little Less Toxic where possible. This kit lives in the garage where it's easily accessible if it's needed in or around the home, but also easy to grab and go on virtually any adventure. What it currently contains is:

- Arnica pellets and/or gel or cream, for pain
- Bentonite clay (small bottle), for many uses including making a poultice to pull poison or venom from sting or bite sites; soothe and treat rashes from poison oak or ivy; mixing with water to help counter digestive upset like diarrhea or vomiting from a viral or bacterial infection, including food

poisoning; and making a protective skin covering for when prolonged sun exposure is unavoidable

- Calendula salve, for burns, chapped skin or lips, rashes, small wounds, and more

- CBD cream and/or drops

- Clotting gauze

- Colloidal silver, handy for managing or preventing many types of infection, ranging from ear, eye, urinary tract, and wound

- Compact emergency blankets

- Couple rolls of cohesive bandages

- Diphenhydramine (antihistamine), chewable and/or liquid for allergic reactions

- Disposable gloves
- Electrolyte packs, to prevent dehydration and provide essential minerals
- Emergency laceration repair/wound closures, including butterfly bandages and other small- to medium-size adhesives that pull wounds closed
- Fever reducer (such as acetaminophen)
- Flashlight, solar-powered and/or crank-powered
- Lighter and waterproof container of matches
- Liposomal vitamin C packs, to help ward off infection; promote tissue repair and wound healing
- Liquid bandage
- Magnesium fire starter
- Organic tampons (for obvious reasons), which can also be handy in other emergency applications like acting as a wound-packing gauze or a fire starter
- Permanent marker, to trace around an infection or bite site to monitor spread; to label wounded sites or appendages for impending emergency personnel; to note time of medical intervention, including medications; to make marks on a trail, and much more
- Pointed tweezers
- Portable charger for phones and devices, charged and ready for use
- Portable, tiny water purifier, using a filter or ozone to remove waterborne

bacteria and parasites in emergencies
- Pulse oximeter
- Quercetin- and bromelain-containing compounds, to help with allergic responses and seasonal allergies
- Roll-up splint that can be cut to size and secured with tape or a bandage
- Small adhesive bandages
- Spray bottle containing HOCl, to sanitize areas; prevent infection in wounds; promote healing; treat bee stings, bug bites, poison oak or ivy, sunburns, virtually all rashes, scrapes, cuts, abrasions, and more
- Surgical scissors
- Thermometer
- Tick remover and identification card
- Tourniquets
- Turmeric and ginger tincture, for pain, inflammation, digestive upset

None of this is medical advice. I can't tell you how and when to use any of this. I know I'd personally rather have it and not need it than need it and not have it. I also prefer to have healthier options, even for emergencies, if and when I can, but in an emergency, obviously, use what you have access to without a second thought. This is not all I'd include in an emergency preparedness kit or go-bag for the home, but all of this would be useful there as well. This kit is grab and go and I'd definitely try to take it with me in an evacuation of the home.

Bathroom Night-Lights

One final tip that has been so helpful for me in the bathroom: We long ago switched to a little salt lamp night-light plugged in in the bathroom. It emits a red-toned light so anyone who has to get up in the night to use the bathroom has a way to see around without getting their circadian rhythm disrupted. I also like to get ready for bed using only that light. Many other night-lights and regular bathroom lights emit brighter, whiter lights that have blue light waves. Blue light tells the body to be alert and awake. Red light doesn't. So, using red light while I get ready for bed (or get up during the night) helps me feel relaxed, fall asleep more easily, and sleep better, too.

the Laundry Room

How many things in life can we count on like the laundry? It doesn't judge you. It doesn't up and leave when you've been less than attentive. It stands by you, no matter how absent you may have been. Day after day, the laundry shows up. Although I do celebrate those eleven seconds of the day when all the laundry is done.

The average family in the United States does six to ten loads of laundry per week and is said to use upwards of five cups of detergent to accomplish this. We are covered by and sleep in those fabrics all day every day. What we use here makes a difference. It impacts our skin, our airways, our insides, our air, and the Earth. This can be a particularly important area to address for those with allergies, eczema, and other health-related concerns.

In this chapter I share helpful tips, tricks, and swaps to keep your clothes and other linens clean and spot-free without the use of harsh chemicals and bleaches. You'll discover which things actually work and which to avoid (and why). I cover ways to prolong the life of your fabrics, tips for keeping your washer and dryer clean and working well, and how to whiten and brighten without ever having to touch a bottle of bleach again. You'll even find out how to remove buildup and odors from preowned, older, or well-loved materials with a simple laundry stripping recipe. In many of these areas, it feels like I need to talk about how grannies had so much of this right and why we should go back to some of their ways!

The Washing Machine

I prefer a top loader. They are less likely to grow mold, thanks to their design. I also enjoy an agitator. (Ahem, not in relationships, but definitely in my washing machine!) I know the clothes can rub up against each other and help each other break free of the grime, but I find an agitator in the mix really helps get the job done. I also appreciate the old style of machine that fills with water so I can soak loads as long as I like. None of these are requirements for doing the laundry well or with fewer toxins. These are just some of my preferences in a machine I use more often than seems reasonable.

Whether you have a top loader or a front loader, leaving the door ajar while not in use helps minimize mold growth. Mold loves to grow in dark, damp places. Let the machine air out as often and as much as possible. Daylight and fresh air are our friends.

It's a good idea to clean your machine periodically, too. I typically do this with up to 1 gallon (3.8 L) of white vinegar in a hot cycle. Organic white vinegar is ideal, if you can find it. Let the machine run for about ten minutes and then sit overnight if possible. If your machine has a setting for self-cleaning, you can use that with the hot water and vinegar. Vinegar will help remove mineral deposits, scale, and buildup from dirt, detergent, grime, and anything in between. Do this quarterly or up to once monthly to help keep the thing that cleans your fabrics clean.

A few general tips for laundry regardless of the machine include:

- Avoid products that say things like "stain resistant" or "water resistant." These usually contain toxic PFAS chemicals.

- Wash new items before use. New items are often treated with things like formaldehyde to maintain perceived freshness or keep them from growing mold or bacteria while spending time in shipping or waiting on a shelf to be purchased.

- Drying materials with natural fibers along with materials with synthetic fibers can increase static in the dryer. If static is a big problem where you live and dryer balls aren't fully doing the trick, try separating the natural-fiber materials from the synthetic before drying.

The Detergent (etc.)

I once tried going the route of making my own laundry soap. But it turns out soap isn't detergent, and detergent is really what's needed to clean clothes effectively. If you're making DIY laundry soap and it works, go you! I tried with all my might for years. Stubborn as I am, I eventually decided that store-bought detergent is the way to go. (True, natural fibers come clean easier with less detergent or without it altogether. I don't know anyone who uses only natural fibers currently. Otherwise, maybe the laundry soap could work there.)

But, of course, not all detergents are created equal. Laundry detergent has long held a top spot on the list of most common household poisoning offenders. The newer pods have intensified this risk. Beyond ingestion threats, the ingredients can contribute to toxic air and environment within the home and other health concerns. If the box says anything like "caution" or "danger," that's a good sign you may not want to invite it into your home. This is another area to look past deceptive language and read the ingredients carefully. Often, the ones labeled "unscented," "sensitive," and "delicate" include some of the most harmful ingredients.

Note: Some of the worst offenders, the ones that really upset me, are the detergents marketed for babies. They claim to be, somehow, safer for babies, yet they're typically loaded with fragrance and other ingredients you'd never knowingly put against your baby's precious body!

I want to stress something here. A clean scent does not equal clean. Scent is problematic for a number of reasons. On its own, it can be made up of any number of less-than-healthy chemicals (see page 15 for more on fragrance). In addition to this, laundry detergents and softeners with fragrance have added ingredients that make the scent bind to the fabrics for longer-lasting scent. It can take eight or more washes to remove detergent and its ingredients from fabrics! The ingredients in the fragrance itself can be toxic. Combine that with synthetic binders and you've got quite a cocktail of junk that can contribute to unhealthy indoor air and health issues. Clean clothes should smell like nothing or like the fabric itself. Not only is fragrance toxic, but it can cover up odors that would otherwise alert you that a product isn't quite clean. Odors like mold, bacterial overgrowth, fecal matter, urine, etc., can hide under the guise of that fresh rain or wildflower bloom aroma.

Some Ingredients I Avoid

- Ammonium lauryl sulfate
- Bleaches
- Dioxane
- Fragrance or parfum
- Nonylphenol ethoxylates (NPEs)
- Oxides like polyalkylene or ethylene
- PEGs
- Petrochemicals
- Sodium laureth sulfate (SLS)
- Synthetic brighteners sometimes labeled "optical brighteners"; formulated to adhere to fabrics and remain there to reflect light and continue to give the appearance of brightness
- Synthetic whiteners

Look beyond claims like "hypoallergenic," "unscented," "free and clear," "sensitive," and the like. The sensitive and unscented versions are often similar to the scented version, but may have added chemicals that help mask the smells of the chemicals still used. Yikes. Marketing claims are there to draw you in; they are often half-truths and can be misleading. The ingredients tell the full story.

I love a powdered detergent with good ingredients and find those work very well. Some have essential oils added for scent, if that helps convince you to make this switch. I make use of the internet and sites like EWG to look at products and individual ingredients to help determine whether it's something I can feel confident bringing into my home. I sometimes add a few drops of essential oils to my detergent before adding it to my washing machine. Tea tree essential oil is my secret weapon for any load with towels or other items, like gym clothes, that can carry their own level of funk.

Fabric Softener

In short, ditch it. This item can be highly problematic when it comes to toxic ingredients and is the biggest offender in the laundry room for fragrance and the chemical binders that make that scent stick to fabrics wash after wash. I used to be a huge fan of this stuff so I get the appeal. It may not be easy to break the habit, but it is worth it.

In place of fabric softener, I now use a little white vinegar in the rinse cycle. If you want to do the same, just pour it right into your washer's fabric softener compartment. A half cup (120 ml) does the trick for a regular load. If your washer is like mine and is without a softener compartment, you can purchase in most laundry aisles a ball designed to release fabric softener. Put your white vinegar in the ball, close it up, and add that right into your washer. This has been my fabric softener for more than a decade. I think you'll find white vinegar can help break down buildup to keep fibers soft. It can also help eliminate odors. And no, your clothes will not smell like a pickle, I promise. Vinegar absorbs odors and then dissipates them. And, as a bonus, it may also help keep mold at bay in your fabrics and in your washer.

Another great option to help soften fibers is wool dryer balls. Pop a few of these in your dryer and they'll last for months. Add extra balls to help combat static cling. Some people also attach safety pins to a few dryer balls for further assistance in eliminating static in drier climates and seasons. I have added a few drops of essential oil, like lavender, to my wool dryer balls for years for a hint of nice scent to my freshly laundered clothes and linens.

Mesh Laundry Bags

I've been using mesh laundry bags for all manner of things for years. They help make my life a little simpler. And not just with laundry!

Here's how mesh laundry bags can help in the laundry room:

- Keep small items like baby socks in bags to keep them from getting trapped in or lost in the wash.

- Place delicate items in these bags to help protect the fabric from damage.

- Place items in these bags that should not go in the dryer to easily identify and remove them from the rest of the washed load.

- Pretreat a stain, then toss the stained item in one of these bags. After washing, check the garment to make sure the stain is eliminated before putting it into the heated dryer. Drying in a hot dryer will further set the stain into the fibers.

Bleach

Bleach was one of the tougher things for me to let go of. I didn't think I could do loads of white laundry without it. It was one of the later things I tried to replace or just remove. I knew it had to go, but kind of ignored how toxic it is so I could hang on to it a bit longer.

Why get rid of it? Well, unfortunately, bleach is an asthmagen, according to the Association of Occupational and Environmental Clinics (AOEC). This means it can contribute to and exacerbate asthma symptoms. It also can contribute to respiratory issues and has been connected to respiratory cancers.

Fortunately, it turns out that bleach is completely unnecessary. I have learned some highly effective, less-toxic, and affordable ways to keep my whites white and clean virtually anything sans chlorine bleach.

I once bought "chlorine-free bleach." When I got it home and looked at the ingredients, I found it's basically peroxide, but costs a lot more. So, I switched to buying bulk peroxide and using that instead of bleach. It works like a charm. A cup or so in a regular load of lights or whites works wonders.

I later learned that fabrics look bright white when new because they're dyed with a touch of blue. The blue reflects more light, causing the white to appear brighter. Have you ever put a brand-new white shirt next to one

that has been washed a number of times? There's a difference. That blue has been washed out. I remembered my mom used liquid bluing in our hair as kids when it turned green after we spent a lot of time in chlorinated water. Well, I found the bluing and tried it with my clothes and, behold: brighter white clothes without bleach!

You might think it would be more chemicals, but most liquid bluing is simply blue iron suspended in water. It has a very small amount of biocide to prevent bacterial growth. One bottle lasts me a year or more. I've been a bluing girl for years now and have not had one instance where I felt the need to return to bleach for laundry. (Or anything else, but more on that in other sections of this book.)

For instructions on how to use liquid bluing for your particular machine, check the package directions or head to the corresponding website. There should be directions for handwashing and for top-loading and front-loading machines. Essentially, it's going to be something like: add ¼ teaspoon bluing to 1 quart (960 ml) of water and mix well. Pour that into your full machine or bleach dispenser. Make sure there aren't blue droplets, because they will stain. Do a test run to be safe. Enjoy brighter, whiter whites, without the bleach.

Treating Stains

If you're addicted to stain removers, fear not: a little pretreat can go a long way toward eliminating the need for other products. Yep, for many stains you can use the detergent you already know and love. Splash on a little water and give it agitation, then let that sit a bit before washing. If you have a stubborn stain on a much-loved garment, there are also stain-treatment options that use ingredients like plant-based enzymes or peroxide-derived ingredients to break down dirt and stains.

I treat stains as soon as possible and let them hang out getting their enzymes broken down for hours (sometimes even days) before laundering. Heat sets stains into fabrics more permanently so always check the item to ensure the stain has been fully lifted before adding it to a hot dryer. If the stain is still there, treat, wash, and check again. Add the stained and treated item to a closed mesh delicates bag before laundering. This way you'll remember it easily and find it before accidentally adding it to the dryer with the rest of the load.

Another great tool for treating stains is the sun. Sunlight naturally lightens stains and brightens whites. It is especially helpful with biological stains (like blood, poop, sweat, and urine). I also want to mention that there's still sunlight on cloudy or rainy days! People often ask me what to do if they have no sun. Here's the scoop: You have sun. Otherwise, it would be nighttime dark all day long. The sun's rays are there and making it light. It can still tackle stains.

This brings me to another laundry lesson I want to touch on: clotheslines. Let's bring them back! I get such joy from the simplicity of hanging our clothes on the line. After a liquid bluing load, I may follow up by hanging the clothes, towels, or sheets out on the line to let the sun really kick up the brightness level another notch. Sunshine and fresh air can also help reduce or eliminate mold, mildew, and lingering chemicals, including fragrance. Imagine tucking yourself in at night smelling the sunshine. Magical. At minimum, it's infinitely better than smelling asthmagens, petrochemicals, and other toxicants.

Laundry Stripping

This is a great method to use for thrifted items, hand-me-downs, cloth diapers, or other items that need a fresh start. In short, it's a process to remove certain residues from fabric.

Over time, fabrics can accumulate buildup that contributes to bacterial overgrowth, dingy appearance, mildew, mold, odors, rough texture, etc. This can be from mineral deposits in the water, detergents, fabric softeners, oil and sebum, dead skin cells, dirt, dust, products, and other factors. Some fabrics can be stripped of these components to help eliminate odor and make them more like they used to be. I do not strip fabrics often, but did become familiar with this practice during my years of cloth diapering.

There are several ways to go about this process but I'm sharing here the method I've had success with. Note that this is not recommended for fabrics that aren't color-safe, are dry clean only, or are very delicate. Use your best judgment. Oh, and always start with clean fabric. It can be wet or dry but should have recently been laundered.

- Top-loading washing machine, bathtub, large basin or bucket, or small pool

- 1 pod GroVia Mighty Bubbles, or ½ to 1 cup each of borax (205 to 409 g) and baking soda (110 to 221 g)

- ½ to 1 cup (112 to 225 g) washing soda (optional)

- Favorite laundry detergent (optional)

- Oxygen boost (optional)

Note: Both cleanser options work with cool water but hot water really helps the powders dissolve and the residue break down. You need enough water to fully submerge the fabrics.

Directions

Fill the basin of your choice with hot water.

Add the Mighty Bubbles (or borax and baking soda).

If you'd like, for extra oomph, add the washing soda, a regular amount of your favorite detergent, and a scoop or two of your favorite oxygen boost.

Add the garments and let soak for several hours, and up to overnight. Stir occasionally, if possible.

Drain, then run the garments through a good rinse cycle (or two) using only water, at a temperature you prefer (I typically use cool). Dry normally.

the Bedroom

It's easy to think of the bedroom as a room where you don't spend much time. In reality, it is one of the most, if not the most, important areas of the home to focus on. If you include the time spent sleeping, about one-third of your day is spent in this room. You're not awake, but time is time. If you add it up, you spend about a third of your life in the bedroom. (In fact, if you work outside the home, you likely spend more time in the bedroom than in any other part of your home.)

Just like the living area and other sections of the home, the materials used here will affect the indoor air quality and, thus, us. We can make mindful choices about anything that comes into this room from the paint to the knickknacks. But the bedroom is also unique, both in some of the materials you encounter and psychologically. After all, the bedroom is where we shut off and our bodies get to work restoring, repairing, and rebalancing. Having less to impede that restoration is a good idea.

In addition, I want to mention that sleep health begins outside the bedroom. Getting adequate sunlight during daylight hours and minimizing other blue light exposure, especially after the sun goes down, can greatly support sleep health. Our overall toxic burden can play a role in sleep health as well. A body out of balance with toxicity can incur inflammation that will impact sleep. An inflamed body typically includes an inflamed brain, and the brain is the sleep master. Poor sleep health impacts overall health as sleep is foundational to recovery.

In addition to what we know about the behaviors outside the bedroom that can affect quality sleep, it is wise to consider what we have, use, and do in our bedrooms, too. In this chapter we will take a closer look at the physical environment of the bedroom and how it can affect our sleep and health. Let's look at some ways to make this space A Little Less Toxic.

Everything for the Bed

The bed is usually the centerpiece of this room. It's more than a pretty place to layer textures and pile on more pillows than certain husbands appreciate. It's also where one-third of our lives are spent, or more, and what you so gracefully smash your face into as you dream the night away. This is the place your body goes into restoration and recovery mode. The materials used, from the bed frame to the mattress, pillows, sheets, blankets, and whatever else you like cozying up with here, are directly against your body with you breathing them in for hours each night. Each piece matters, and cumulatively, they can have a big impact on your overall well-being.

Mattress

Let's take a look at the bed (after all, it puts the "bed" in bedroom!) starting with the mattress. When it was time to replace our mattress, we lived in denial for a while and slept clinging to the very edge to avoid sleeping in the pit in the center. During this time, I did shop around for a quality mattress that would be comfortable, supportive, and long lasting. Of course, I wanted it to be A Little Less Toxic, if possible. I learned that most conventional mattresses these days are made with materials such as adhesives, flame retardants, foam, metal coils, polyester, synthetic latex, and vinyl. Many manufacturers also use wool or cotton to varying degrees, but those do not make up the bulk of the product. Although foam and latex seem benign, they're commonly made with some not so lovely materials and processes.

Foam has become increasingly common in mattresses and mattress toppers as it is lightweight and inexpensive to produce. Memory foam, in particular, is wildly popular. Both memory foam and polyurethane foam are petroleum based though. Memory foams are polyurethane foams with additional chemicals that make the foam slow to respond and give that well-known memory foam feel. Even "plant-based" foams are mostly polyurethane with some percentage of plant-based foam incorporated into the material. This means the vast majority of us spend 33 percent of our lives on what is, essentially, a plastic. Not only that, but polyurethane is a byproduct of petroleum, a crude oil. The end product is highly flammable and so will be heavily treated with flame retardants.

A California state law, enacted in 1975 and called TB 117, requires flame retardants to be used in many home furnishings and, especially, mattresses. Manufacturers across the United States, and many internationally, adopted this policy. All mattresses using any foam were to contain flame retardants. The law has been updated as recently as 2014 (TB 117 2013) to decrease the use of these flame retardants as we learn about their potential hazards to health. Although use of these chemicals in many furniture items and fabrics is lessening, mattresses are not included in the update. The National Institutes of Health (NIH) recognizes flame retardants as endocrine mimickers.

Flame-retardant chemicals are something I want to keep out of my home as best I'm able, but especially out of my bed. The chemicals used to alter the crude oil and turn it into a foam, in combination with chemical adhesives and the flame retardants used, can make this a less-than-healthy option on which to spend a large chunk of our lives.

As with all things, there are lots of clever marketing tactics, claims, and supposed certifications thrown around that can be overwhelming and confusing. I've included an up-to-date list of some certifications that actually mean something to help you when mattress and bedding shopping (see 20). When it comes time to replace a mattress in your home, these are some things you can look for to help determine what fits your needs and budget.

There are several great mattress brands on the market at the time of writing and more emerging at varying price points to meet a wide range of budgets. I looked for the best bang for the buck that would fit our budget rather than going for the absolute best or most expensive mattress choice. I found you do not have to sacrifice comfort or durability for health. Our mattress is made of natural organic latex, organic wool, and organic cotton and without the use of any polyester, polyurethane, fire retardants, or adhesives—and it did not cost substantially more than a good-quality mattress without these features.

If a whole mattress is not in the budget, or it's not time to replace yours, a good option might be a mattress topper. A few inches of a mattress topper can create some space between you and the mattress underneath. It can also block some of the off-gassing and help maintain healthier indoor air. Natural latex and wool are great options used by many brands for toppers.

a healthier home

132

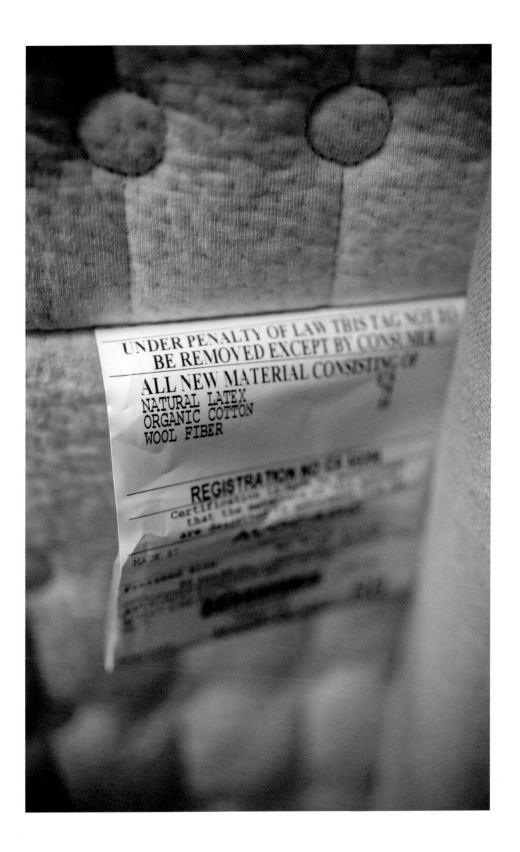

Whether or not you have a low-tox mattress or topper, a protective covering on your mattress is a way to help make the bedroom a healthier space. A protector can be a barrier against spills and accidents, which will prolong the life of your mattress and save you the headache of damage to the mattress. (Completely drying the inside of a mattress after a spill is virtually impossible and odds are mold and unwanted bacteria will develop inside the mattress where you cannot see it, remove it, or treat it. This can contribute to poor air quality as well as breathing and other health issues.)

A good protective cover can save you that unwanted scenario and can also (should also!) be washed regularly. Washing will help combat dust mites and their feces, which are highly culpable in allergies, asthma, and other respiratory issues. It will also keep dead skin cells, sweat, and other unwanted matter from collecting on and penetrating your mattress. The

ability to remove and wash this covering means removing those gross things from your bed before nuzzling your face and body against them for hours.

There are many options available for covers. Unfortunately, many brands are reluctant to list what membrane material is used between the outer organic materials. Even the low-tox brands typically use a TPU (thermoplastic polyurethane) or similar material that will prevent liquid from penetrating. If a brand does not state what materials are used, I either ask for that information or, more commonly, shop for a brand that is more transparent instead. I feel good about a thin layer of TPU, especially when it's met certification like MADE SAFE®, as it's what gets the job done and will help keep my mattress in good condition and healthier longer. If you want to avoid TPU, wool is a good option for a mattress protector but is not waterproof and cannot be washed like other toppers.

Pillows

Pillows can be a great swap to make the bedroom and your sleep environment healthier. Whether or not you replace the entire mattress, updating to pillows with low-tox materials can support your health and the environment within your bedroom and home. Pillows are much more affordable to replace than an entire mattress. They are also right up against your face and respiratory input locations (for one-third of your life). Due to its proximity to your body and the duration of time there, it's a good idea to minimize toxins in this item.

The same certifications for mattresses apply to pillows and can be helpful tools in pillow shopping. Sleep position, body composition, and preference should all be considered when determining the best pillow for you. No matter what pillow you have or buy, my top tips are to keep them covered, launder all coverings at least every seven to ten days, and expose them to fresh air regularly. An open window letting in fresh air and letting out indoor air does a lot of good for pillows, too.

COMMON PILLOW PROBLEMS

Allergens, including dust mites, fungi, and mold: This problem is another reminder to use a protector over your bedding materials. Dust mites plus their dander and feces can penetrate the surface of your pillows and take up residence in that thing you smash your face into and breathe on all night. Not only is this disgusting to think about but it can also be a major contributor to allergies and respiratory issues, including sinusitis and asthma. This is also true of many types of fungi as well as mold and the mycotoxins mold can produce. Sweat and drool only make things worse. Just like I recommend doing with your mattress, invest in a quality pillow protector that will serve as a protective barrier between your pillow and these unwanted guests. Wash the cover regularly in hot water and a good detergent. This will help your pillow last longer and make any pillow a healthier material to sleep on and snuggle with.

Flame retardants: Yep, they're used heavily in pillows, too. Just like the foams used in mattresses, the polyurethane used to compose the majority of pillows on the market today is a byproduct of petroleum and contains flame retardant. According to the EPA and EWG, polyurethane contains PBDEs, which have been linked to hormone disruption as well as other health concerns including bioaccumulation (see page 19 for more about flame retardants and PBDEs).

Formaldehyde: A hypoallergenic or wrinkle-free claim is often an indicator that formaldehyde has been used. Many fabrics are treated with formaldehyde before hitting shelves to help them feel and appear fresh longer—and pillows are no exception.

Fragrance: Because most pillows are created using many chemical compounds and treatments, there will often be chemical-laden perfumes, fragrances, and/or deodorizers used to offset those smells. It's frustrating to see chemicals to counter chemicals.

VOCs: Due to the items discussed here, and more, pillows can be a likely source of VOCs (see page 20 for more on this).

If you're considering a memory foam pillow the concerns are similar to those for mattresses; see page 131 for information about memory foam and other forms of foam and why those are materials I avoid. Cooling pillows are also typically made with foams such as those I've discussed as well as other man-made gels—all composed of potentially toxic materials. Some organic fibers, like wool and linen, naturally regulate temperature well and can be a great alternative.

Other pillow materials may include down feathers, or down alternatives (typically made with polyester, another petroleum derivative) for those with allergies or for a lower-cost option with a similar feel. Although down feathers are a more natural material to use, some manufacturers treat the feathers with some rather unnatural stuff that can include various glues to create specific textures or desired weight. Many are also coated with

antifungal and/or antibacterial substances. The manufacturer should be able to provide transparency about what is used in its pillow materials as well as processing and manufacturing information. (Reluctance to provide that information can be a red flag.)

Natural fibers tend to be less toxic, especially when we keep the previously mentioned items in mind. The outer shell or cover is as important as the inner fill. As with all things, inspect labels and claims. Ask questions if transparency is lacking, or find a brand that proudly discloses materials and practices.

Some Healthier Pillow Materials

- **Kapok:** From the seeds of the kapok tree; soft, lightweight, airy, sustainable, durable, naturally hypoallergenic, mold resistant, and water resistant

- **Natural latex:** Soft, supportive, moldable; great alternative to memory foam or an option for those with wool or feather allergies

- **Organic cotton:** Lightweight, sustainable, soft, durable; made in various densities and fullness; can be used in fill as well as the shell

- **Organic wool:** Supportive, soft, breathable, temperature regulating, naturally flame resistant and dust mite resistant

Bedding

At the risk of sounding like a broken record: Just like the mattress and pillows, bedding can be treated with pesticides, herbicides, formaldehyde, and other chemicals. Some of the worst offenders have claims like "wrinkle-free," "easycare," "anti-static," "stain repellent," "antimicrobial," and "shrinkage-free." To achieve those claims, the fibers are typically treated with various chemicals. Synthetic and mixed or blended fibers, which can feel quite soft, are often chemically treated to achieve certain textures at a lower cost to the manufacturer. Acrylic, nylon, and polyester are petroleum byproducts—they're essentially plastic. Being snuggled up against any of that for eight hours every single day is not ideal.

For duvets and duvet cover, sheets and pillowcases, quilts, throws, etc., natural fibers are a healthier option. Organic cotton is a great option for bed linens (though keep in mind what we already discussed about cotton; see page 84). Other natural fibers to consider for breathable and sleep-supportive bedding include my personal favorites, linen and bamboo. Both are breathable and temperature regulating while being durable, sustainable, and A Little Less Toxic. Silk and wool can also be okay, but both tend to be higher maintenance for care. Again, utilize reliable certifications, such as MADE SAFE®, OEKO-TEX®, and GOTS, which can help assure that even the dyes used are safer for your bed, home, and life, to help you find an option that fits your preferences, needs, and budget.

Duvet Hack

Found your new duvet cover but struggling to put it on? Try this!

1 Lay your duvet over the bed.

2 Lay your duvet cover directly on top of the duvet, inside-out, with the opening at the foot of the bed.

3 Tie any corners, if your duvet or cover has them.

4 Begin rolling the duvet and duvet cover together, like a wrap from your local café, starting at the head of the bed and working toward the opening at the foot of the bed.

5 Once the duvet and cover are all rolled down to the foot of the bed, invert the cover over the duvet at each of the two exposed corners.

6 Unroll and experience absolute magic.

7 Fasten any buttons or ties and enjoy!

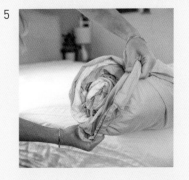

the bedroom

More than Materials

No matter what you have in your sleeping space, the environment you create is just as important as the materials. In other words, you can use all nontoxic materials, but if you do not incorporate some basic smart sleep principles and practices, you may not get the quality rest your body needs to restore and repair. Let's look at some practices, principles, and tools to help support quality of sleep.

The physical environment should be relaxing. Eliminating clutter is both aesthetically pleasing and calming to the nerves. Less clutter will also help keep dust, which we know is toxic, at bay. Take the time to tidy and try to keep your sleep space a calm place of retreat. Consider the decor. It can reflect whatever your personal style is, but should not be the brightest room in the home. Colors, decorations, fabrics, and lighting should evoke feelings of rest and relaxation.

Speaking of lighting, blackout shades aren't my favorite because I try to welcome natural light into my home to support circadian rhythms. However, they might be appropriate for those who work night shifts, people who live in areas with lots of streetlight outside the bedroom, etc. I generally feel the same way about sleep masks, but I do use one on occasion, especially if I need a midday reboot. For lamps and overhead lighting, I try not to use those much in the evening. When we do, I prefer dim, warm light with more red undertones than blue, again to support circadian rhythm, which is so crucial to quality sleep and overall health. Candlelight is even better (and sexier!).

Blue Light and Electronics

I admit, at first I thought "blue light" was a gimmick thanks to shades people were raving about in commercials on the Venice boardwalk in the 1980s—complete with a 1-800 number scrawled across the lower screen. It turns out, they were just ahead of their time. These days we're inundated by blue light, not only from lighting but also screens, and it really can have a negative impact on sleep and well-being. Blue light can affect alertness, sleep cycles, hormone production, and more. I do not know of anything that impacts sleep more than light.

Most blue light exposure comes from the sun. That exposure occurs naturally during hours we're typically awake, which is ideal because blue light makes us feel alert. During the day, blue light is our friend and can improve attention and performance. It also works with our built-in circadian rhythm and, when blue light is received during appropriate hours, can help prepare us for better sleep at night. In the evening though, it's a good idea to limit the amount of blue light we're exposed to. Ways to do this can include using lighting with dimmers or warmer, redder tones; using less artificial light, especially fluorescent and LED bulbs; using candles for evening lighting; turning off screens close to bedtime, including TV, computer, laptop, phone, or tablet; and using blue light–mitigating eyewear. If you must use electronics close to bedtime, many devices have settings to make the screen display with more red waves and fewer blue ones, which may be beneficial to you. If you enjoy reading in bed, I have found booklights with warm, dark orange or red, non-LED light to be a great way to enjoy the activity but with less negative effects on sleep quality than reading on a screen.

While on the topic of electronic devices, let's examine the rabbit hole of EMFs. Electromagnetic fields are everywhere today and we cannot completely avoid them. Any and every device that uses electricity, inevitably, emits some EMFs. The amount can vary, but even a table lamp can, in some cases, be a powerful source of EMF waves. There is more and more emerging research on the potential effects of EMFs on our health, including topics like cancer, inflammatory diseases, and more. My thinking is, it's not totally avoidable, so I don't panic about it. Stress can be much more harmful. I do try to be mindful and limit or mitigate when and where I'm able to though. For EMFs, the general rule is to limit amount and increase distance.

Ways to Minimize EMF Exposure

- Avoid fluorescent or halogen lighting.

- Convert smart meters on the home back to analog, if possible.

- Get some grounding in throughout the day when you're able, through direct contact with the Earth, by gardening, taking a barefoot stroll on the grass or beach, or anything in between.

- Hardwire the home.

- Leave Bluetooth off or out of the room, as much as possible.

- Leave your phone out of the room, or turn it to airplane mode if kept in the room.

- Position the bed in the room as far away from the meter and electrical boxes, especially if they are located on the same walls as the bedroom.

- Take note of the proximity to power lines in the neighborhood. If possible, position beds farther away from these.

- Turn off Wi-Fi routers during sleep hours; there are devices that can do this for you at set times.

- Unplug any devices not in use.

- Use grounding mats and other accessories.

- Utilize mitigating equipment, like Faraday cages for routers, harmonizing devices, etc.

Mouth Tape

I understand this is a bizarre concept if you've never heard of it (I remember what I thought when I discovered it). I also get some strange reactions when I share that this is what I do and the effect it's had on my sleep.

Mouth taping is a simple way to make sure you breathe through your nose while asleep. I tried it for the first time after reading about potential benefits.

The first moment my mouth was taped, I felt a panic. After a few seconds of reminding myself no harm was coming to me, I forgot it was even there. I dozed off and got incredible sleep. I woke without a nasty taste in my mouth, without dry mouth, and feeling *good*. I've continued to mouth tape most nights. And those nights I doze off before I get my tape on? I wake up regretting it.

How can something as simple as a piece of tape improve sleep? It's because mouth breathing can contribute to many health issues, including dry mouth, which can contribute to high acidity and poorly protected teeth, leading to cavities. It can disrupt the oral microbiome, leading to an imbalance in beneficial microbes, creating an environment for opportunistic pathogens to thrive (see page 93 for more on the oral microbiome and oral health). Mouth breathing has also been linked to abnormal facial growth, cognitive impairment, growth disorders, misaligned teeth, poor sleep, symptoms akin to those present in ADHD, and more.

There are some tapes specifically designed for this purpose, but I use inexpensive surgical tape. Before dozing off, I apply my lip balm, relax my mouth while my lips are pressed together, and place a little strip of tape over my mouth, vertically. This allows me to talk, if needed, take sips of water through a straw, and provides a space to insert my thermometer to take my temperature upon waking (fertility awareness).

Potential Benefits of Mouth Taping

- Better remineralization
- Improved quality of sleep
- Lower risk of cavities
- Reduced snoring
- Reduction of dry mouth
- Reduction of teeth grinding
- Support for the oral microbiome

In addition to the benefits just listed, mouth taping improves nitric oxide levels which can help:

- Enhance memory and learning
- Improve immune/gut function
- Improve sleep quality
- Improve symptoms of anxiety and depression
- Increase endurance and strength
- Promote weight loss
- Reduce heart disease risk
- Regulate blood pressure
- Regulate inflammatory response
- Relieve pain

the bedroom

Bedroom Activities

I'm going there. Let's chat about sexy time and what we can do to make that part of our life A Little Less Toxic. From candles to contraceptives, we have options to make this a healthier part of our lives, too.

Candles

I used to be a big scented-candle fan. I love good smells and the cozy feel a candle can give off. But once I learned how problematic fragrance and other candle components can be, I went candleless for years. The ingredient "fragrance" can contain many, many ingredients that need not be disclosed. Oftentimes, those ingredients will include chemicals such as phthalates, which help the scent linger or stick and that are also reported to be endocrine disruptors (see more about this topic on page 25).

Most candles on the market are made with some amount of paraffin wax, which will have within it other substances we could benefit from keeping out of our homes and bedrooms. Paraffin often contains compounds such as benzene and toluene, which are known carcinogens and have also been associated with respiratory issues, allergies, asthma, and some skin conditions. The wick can be another area of concern as many are pesticide-laden cotton and may even include lead.

What I avoid in a candle: Bleached cotton wicks, fragrance, paraffin, petrochemicals

What I look for in a candle: Beeswax, coconut, or soy wax; fragrance-free or scented with safer plant extracts or essential oils; lead-free unbleached cotton or unprocessed wooden wicks

I was so happy when I learned that plain and pure beeswax candles can actually help clean the air. This is because beeswax candles can release negative ions into the air as they burn. The negative ions can counter the positive ions of indoor air contaminants and neutralize them. Neutralized ions are sucked back into the burning candle, or fall to the ground, helping purify the air in the process. (Some air purifiers use negative ion technology to help purify air as well.)

I also use safer scented candles, many of which are blends, like beeswax plus coconut oil. I love some scented candles with essential oils or with nontoxic plant extracts, without reproductive toxins, parabens, phthalates, endocrine disruptors, or carcinogens. They do exist, and many work amazingly and smell fantastic.

Contraceptive Options

As a former hormonal birth control user for many years, I didn't find it easy to make the switch to a more holistic approach. I eventually made the switch years ago, for many reasons, and I'm glad I did. Since doing so, I've spent hours seeking products and methods that would best support my goals for family planning as well as my health.

The main method I use is the fertility awareness method, also known as natural family planning. This involves monitoring the body for changes that indicate times the body is fertile in order to become or prevent becoming pregnant. This may include tracking body temperature upon waking daily (known as basal body temperature), tracking changes in cervical mucus, and noticing other cyclical changes.

There are several ways of collecting this data and tracking that include a thermometer and a paper journal, a thermometer and an app on a personal mobile device, or fancy gadgets that take your temperature and track the data alongside science-backed algorithms to predict fertile windows with extremely high accuracy and efficacy. My husband and I have been using such a device for several years now, successfully, and I have found it useful in helping me understand my body and cycles better as well.

We do use condoms for extra protection during fertile windows when we are trying to avoid pregnancy. Common condom ingredients include parabens, which can be estrogen mimickers, can harm beneficial bacteria and disrupt your very important microbiome, may be linked to some cancers, can disrupt hormones, and may present reproductive, immune, and neurological toxicity. Other ingredients present in most condoms that I prefer to avoid include nonoxynol-9, nitrosamines, glycerin, casein, and benzocaine. Fortunately, there are several brands making less-toxic condom options that refrain from using any of these ingredients.

Lube

Many manufacturers of these products use ingredients I find concerning and not something I want in such a sensitive area. Parabens, including butylparaben, ethylparaben, methylparaben, and propylparaben, are commonly used as synthetic preservatives. Parabens may disrupt hormones as they can mimic estrogen. Petrochemical-based products, such as petroleum jelly, can have negative health effects as well. Other common ingredients I prefer to keep away from include cyclomethicone, fragrance, natural or synthetic flavors, phenoxyethanol, polysorbates, and propylene glycol.

As consumers become more aware of ingredients and spend money on healthier products, we see more companies make products with fewer unwanted ingredients. There are store-bought options without parabens and some of the other ingredients of concern, though at the time of writing it might be easier to search online. As with all things, my recommendation is to read the ingredients on these items before purchasing anything. Until we found a better lubricant with good ingredients, we used coconut oil (but it is not good to use with latex condoms). Of course, good old-fashioned saliva works, too.

Note: What about other items used for pleasure? For all the reasons listed many times in this book, and because these items are in such close contact with highly sensitive areas of the body, it would be wise to opt for healthier materials instead of those with plastics, "jelly rubber," PVC, BPA, BPS, glues, elastomers, silicone blends, fragrance, toxic dyes, and flavoring. Some less-toxic materials include medical-grade silicone, glass, pure and solid crystal, and medical-grade stainless steel.

Outside *the* Home

‹‹‹

No matter what type of home we reside in, I want to emphasize the importance of getting outside of those doors of yours. Fresh air and sunshine can do a world of good for our mood and our bodies. Whether it's in your own outdoor space, yard, or garden, or a public space, get outside regularly. Daily, if you're able. Even in freezing weather or on the grayest of days, the sun's rays are, indeed, illuminating the Earth and that fresh air and sunlight can do so much good for your health and well-being. Even if for just three minutes, it truly makes a difference.

‹‹‹

The light and warmth from the sun have the ability to interact with our bodies on a cellular level. There are endless studies on the benefits of sunshine. A very well-recognized benefit is vitamin D. Natural vitamin D has been associated with many facets of overall health, including bone and heart health, immune function, mental health, and resistance to infections and chronic conditions. Meanwhile, insufficient levels of vitamin D, which many, if not most, people deal with, are associated with a whole host of health concerns, including chronic pain, depression, fatigue, insomnia, low immune function, osteoporosis, skin disorders, susceptibility to infectious disease, and more. The sun is an important tool for our health. Somewhere along the way, many of us have learned to fear the sun when I believe a healthy respect for it would be much more beneficial. The sun provides light and contributes to life for all living things, including us. There is much benefit that can be derived from regular and healthy exposure to the sun. It is the imbalanced relationship with the sun that can lead to harm. Both too little and too much sunshine can lead to unhealthy consequences for the body. What I aim to do is gain benefit from the sun while making choices that minimize potential harm or damage.

Get Outside!

We are not moles or groundhogs. Humans are designed to live above ground and that will mean almost daily sun exposure. If we're meant to live above ground and we're not nocturnal, should we hide from and fear the sun? In all of human history, people are getting less sun exposure than ever, while we're seeing higher and higher rates of cancers including those attributed to sun exposure, like melanomas. We are indoors most of the day and sometimes all day every day, yet skin cancers are rampant. There are many factors I ponder regarding this issue. We are designed to need the sun and it regulates important processes of the body. We are being told that the sun is dangerous. The rays of today may reach us differently than they did our ancestors for a number of reasons including the atmosphere.

I also think it's important to consider how our lifestyle contributes to this issue. What we ingest might alter how we respond to sunlight. Some foods, such as those high in antioxidants, vitamins C or K, lycopene and others, may help the skin receive benefits from the sun while also helping protect it from potential damage. If this is true, it's not difficult to understand that eating fewer of those types of foods can negatively affect our bodies' ability to interact with UV rays. It's also reasonable to believe some foods may interfere with our skin and its relationship with sunlight. What we use on and around our bodies can also contribute to interference with a healthy relationship with sunshine. Many of these same foods and products that can interfere come with their own risk as well. Many conventional topical sunscreens have ingredients that are known carcinogens. I believe we can mitigate harm without incurring more harm with a mindful approach.

Sun Protection

I could go on and on about the sun and how it should not be feared, but respected and utilized with a healthy approach. Two issues I see with an imbalanced approach to living with the sun are insufficient exposure to the sun and the overuse of sunscreen as it impairs our bodies' ability to produce vitamin D. Even worse is the overuse of those products with ingredients that carry additional health risks. I encourage you to keep learning about this subject. It's fascinating!

I'll stop there but I want to leave you with some of my balanced approach to sunshine for maximum benefit and minimal harm:

- Aim for some direct sunlight on your skin daily. For fair skin, ten to fifteen minutes may suffice; for more melanated skin, more time may be necessary to produce sufficient vitamin D—some suggest up to 40 minutes. This will vary for each individual.

- Early morning sun exposure is my favorite. In addition to vitamin D–producing benefits, early morning sun exposure can increase melatonin production for better sleep at night. It can also increase dopamine, the feel-good neurotransmitter.

- Nourish well inside and out. Consume varied whole foods to help your body function its best and be resilient in the sunshine and everywhere.

- Try an app that helps you know whether you're getting enough sunlight for optimal vitamin D. My current favorite is D Minder.

- Avoid the high sun hours, around 11 a.m. through 3 p.m., or use more protection, like clothing, umbrellas, etc., during this time.

 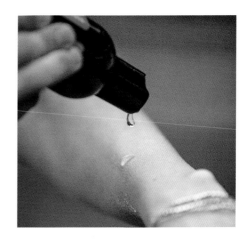

- Protective clothing or coverage can be useful. I love a good hat or visor. Long, lightweight clothing has been used for centuries during long hours of sun exposure. Linen has been a widely popular material for ages; it is breathable and temperature regulating.

- Topical sunscreen: For times of need, I prefer a physical sunscreen to a chemical one, even when it comes to creams and lotions. I choose sunscreens whose active ingredients include zinc and/or titanium oxide. I avoid chemicals that may absorb into the bloodstream, like oxybenzone and octinoxate. I don't find them necessary with the many other healthier alternatives on the market. Even with a mineral sunscreen, it's important to read the ingredients. I avoid ingredients like fragrance and even essential oils, as some are photosensitive.

- Pay attention to your body. A sunburn is your body's warning sign.

- Remember that the sun's rays are making it NOT NIGHT and even gray days are full of the sun's rays.

- Stay hydrated. Always. And especially on hotter days

For after-sun care, I love a good hypochlorous acid spray or aloe. Owning an aloe plant can come in handy for all sorts of things, including sunburns. A lukewarm bath with a tied-off sock full of oats can also be soothing to sunburned skin as well as many other skin irritations.

Insect Protection

On the topic of getting outside, we often have the issue of insects to deal with. There are many ways to live in the world with these critters without incurring harm to our bodies or our environment.

I have found quite a few brands of insect repellent sprays and creams that are less toxic but really work. They don't make me cough and splutter and they have kept unwanted visitors from pestering my ears with their incessant buzzing, or feasting on my blood. They utilize the power of plants that pests hate, even though I think they're delightful. These may include the potent essential oils of cedarwood, citronella, lemongrass, peppermint, and others. These bugs don't know what they're missing. A less-toxic synthetic that works great is picaridin. It's very effective against ticks, mosquitoes, and chiggers. There are a few brands using this ingredient alongside other low-tox ingredients. I've also made my own insect repellent by adding a few drops of essential oil blends, like those listed previously, in carrier oils like jojoba as a topical treatment or in a spray bottle with water and witch hazel.

Grounding

While we're outside, let's amp up the health benefits with some grounding. If you've ever had an EKG, ECG, or similar, you know that we, indeed, have electrical signals throughout our bodies helping them function properly. We are bioelectric beings. The Earth also uses electricity. Grounding, or earthing, as it is sometimes called, is simply putting the body in direct contact with the Earth. This can be bare feet on the grass, sand, or soil, hands touching plants, and just about anything in between. Skin touching Earth. In a nutshell, people are bioelectric beings carrying lots of positively charged electrons. The Earth is loaded with negatively charged or free electrons. If you recall ever being shocked by a doorknob or car door, you know that skin can act as a conductor of electricity. When we put our bodies in direct contact with the Earth, it can quite literally help ground us, similar to how electrical outlets have a grounding element included. The Earth's abundance of negative electrons can help create a more stable bioelectrical environment internally as electrical conductivity exists within our bodies' systems. Modern living has distanced us from this source of negative charge that can help us be in better balance. Even modern shoes have interrupted this process. Shoe soles used to be more natural

materials, like leather, which allow for conduction of electricity. Synthetic materials and even rubber block this process. Being more mindful about getting ourselves grounded has many potential health benefits. Studies have been lacking on this topic, but more are surfacing and revealing what many experience. Direct contact with the Earth may contribute to greater health. Don't overthink this. Kick off your shoes outside when you're able. Get in direct contact with nature more regularly. Get your hands dirty. Be more like a kid!

Potential Benefits of Grounding

- Better energy
- Decreased pain
- Decreased stress hormones, like cortisol
- Faster healing
- Improved sleep
- Reduced Inflammation

Ways to Ground

- Garden, or touch trees or plants with your bare hands.
- Take an Epsom salts bath. Water should increase conductivity and the bath is (often) connected to metal piping that is connected to . . . the ground! Plastic piping will interrupt the grounding here.

- Walk or stand barefoot on grass, soil, sand, untreated concrete, natural stone, gravel, snow.

- Wear leather-soled shoes, when possible.

- Wet places, like hot springs, lakes, ocean, and rivers, may have even greater benefits.

There are some pretty cool tools being invented to be able to ground more indoors, including mats for the bed, grounding sheets, socks, shoes, etc. Some may be gimmicks, and some may have benefit. Do a little digging before taking the financial plunge with these devices. The free stuff, like bare feet, even for 10 minutes a day, can make a positive impact. Aim for 30 minutes or more when you're able, but don't discount the difference even a few minutes can make.

The Garden

In our yard, we welcome dandelions and clovers. I know weeds aren't very popular. Some of the plants commonly hated and frequently removed, often at the expense of our health, include those that are beneficial to very important neighbors. There has been a problem with pollinator decline for some time. This is a big problem for every living thing that eats as bees, butterflies, and other pollinators are centric to our food supply. Herbivores survive off plants. Plants can't continue to repopulate without being pollinated. Omnivores also need the plants, of course. But omnivores and carnivores alike need the herbivores to be able to live to have their needs met as well. All things that eat need plants in one way or another and plants need pollinators. Pollinators love clover and dandelions and many other plants we consider pests. Once I learned to respect the grass invaders for what they are, I started seeing them as beautiful, welcomed guests, not eyesores and pests. Much to the chagrin of a few feet that suffered stings (and survived), we keep some "weeds" thriving in our grass.

Another aspect I find fascinating is that overgrowth of weeds may suggest an imbalance in the terrain. So similar to our bodies! A healthy balanced turf will keep invaders out much better than one overmedicated, undernourished, and neglected. It's like that concept of not being able to medicate or supplement your way out of an unhealthy diet or lifestyle. This applies to the Earth and the garden, too.

For lawn care, proper watering is helpful. There are some great products that use less-toxic ingredients to help feed and nourish the soil and lawn or garden, too. Some use ingredients like iron, volcanic ash, seaweed, phosphorus, molasses, and broken-down igneous rocks like scoria to feed the good and/or to deter the unwanted. Chemicals don't just go away. They wash into the soil. Some absorb into the plants themselves. They enter the air we breathe. Using more natural ingredients that are less risky to our health and environment, and using less of those known to be carcinogens, or that pose other potential health risks, is better for the Earth, better for your garden, and better for you and your family. And, they happen to work really well for us and so many others who've made the switch.

Pest Control

Pests can be indoors or outdoors. For pests in the garden or around the home I have a few less-toxic tricks up my sleeve. First, though, a reminder that an abundance of unwanted living things can be the result of an imbalanced environment. Adding more toxins to the mix is rarely the answer. It may pop a quick plug over the leak, but the problem will return. Before I get into some treatments for when pests make their uninvited house call, let's go over some basics to help delay that visit.

- Clean/maintain surfaces regularly. Vinegar is a natural insect deterrent so cleaning with my DIY ALLT Multipurpose Cleaner (see page 72) containing lemon-infused vinegar can help, but any cleaning helps. Dusting regularly is important, too. Cobwebs make pests think places are more inviting and cozy.

- Consider the microbes. Healthy and beneficial microbes in, around, and outside the home help keep the detrimental microbes in check. Overuse of sanitizers, pesticides, and other toxic things that kill may contribute to a greater imbalance and more pest problems down the road.

- Keep a tidy environment. Inside and out. Clutter leads to lots of hiding places for dust, insects, mold, and other pests. It's also hard to clean around clutter.

- Mind the crumbs. That one speck of food that fell unnoticed can be like a beacon of light to ants, mice, roaches, and other things that make my skin crawl. Nothing a decent broom can't manage.

- Move very ripe fruit to a refrigerator, or keep it covered with a tightly woven mesh produce bag to keep the fruit flies and others from taking up residence.

Now, some tools.

DIATOMACEOUS EARTH

This gray powder is made from fossilized water plants. It is naturally occurring and loaded with silica. It acts as a mineral-based pesticide that can be effective against pests like ants, aphids, bedbugs, earwigs, mites, roaches, slugs, and snails. Opt for food-grade diatomaceous earth—I keep a big bag in the cupboard at all times. You can sprinkle this around the garden or home to deter pests. Be careful not to inhale it as it can be dangerous. Wearing a dust mask while using it is a good idea. One of my favorite ways to apply diatomaceous earth is with a turkey baster. Add some DE to a bowl or bottle and suck it up into the turkey baster, then squirt out a line of DE around the perimeter of the home or plants or any place you are trying to keep pests out of.

PEPPERMINT ESSENTIAL OIL

Many insects and rodents, including ants, mice, and spiders, find the scent of peppermint repulsive. Another reason I dislike them. I have used peppermint oil successfully to tell these critters to take a hike on many occasions. I have two methods that are easy and effective.

1 Add a few drops of peppermint essential oil to a spray bottle full of water. Spray down clean surfaces a few times a day and especially at night.

2 Drop some peppermint essential oil onto some cotton balls and place these around the home. For mice, placing these up high can help drive mice down to where traps can be laid. We have used a catch and release–style trap the few times we have needed one in our home.

NEEM OIL

This oil is typically made from cold pressing the seeds of the neem tree. As a highly concentrated oil with its unique properties and compounds, it functions as a natural insecticide. Neem oil can be a less-toxic and highly effective way to kill and deter pests in the yard or garden, including aphids, beetles, slugs, and upwards of two hundred other potential garden bandits. It's best to use during cooler times of the day and avoid times when direct sunlight is on the treated parts of the plant. Neem oil may also prevent fungal growth on plants. It is also useful in deterring mosquitoes. If you live in an area with high mosquito traffic, treating your yard with neem may help protect all who reside there from those blood suckers.

CAYENNE PEPPER

Cayenne is another natural insecticide. Small children, many family members, and people with weaker taste buds than mine all over the world reject the heat provided by the capsaicin in this pepper. Many insects hate it, too, and it can deter many pests in the garden, including ants, aphids, and lace bugs. Even racoons and other unwelcome nighttime garden raiders are offended by cayenne and it may help keep them at bay. It does not harm any plants that I'm aware of. I use cayenne on our hibiscus plants regularly to keep aphids at bay. Multiple or regular applications may be necessary.

1 Fill a 16-ounce (480 ml) spray bottle with water, add a pinch of cayenne, and a drop or two of dish soap. Cover, give it a shake, and spray any plant, as often as needed.

Compost

This is a relatively new add for me and was something that overwhelmed me a bit, for no good reason. Food scraps and some other organic matter from your home can bypass the dump and make lush, rich soil. It's like magic. This process can get involved and complex, or you can keep it really simple. We take scraps like banana peels, eggshells, potato peels, strawberry tops, and more that would otherwise end up in the garbage can and put them in a compost bin in the sun out back. We rotate the drum every few days. In a matter of weeks to months, our garbage becomes beautiful earth we use in the garden, around trees, plants, or anywhere, really. When we're ready to upgrade, we'll either get a second barrel or a barrel with two chambers so one can be added to while the other breaks down into that good stuff. Compost helps minimize waste, improves soil, and can reduce any need for synthetic fertilizers. Plus, it's fun seeing our garbage turn into useful and healthy earth.

Watering

For watering the lawn and garden, there are really cool filters that you can twist onto your spigot or hose to reduce toxins like chemical pesticides, chloramine, chlorine, heavy metals, volatile compounds, and other contaminants. I have one we really like and it only needs to be replaced about once a year. These filters are becoming more common and available but may have to be ordered online. I love having this tool for reducing toxins in our yard and environment but also just for reducing how much gets put back into the world.

Before I had the filter, or for using a hose without it, to fill the kids' little pool out back on hot days, I used the ascorbic acid trick to neutralize chlorine (see page 84 for more on this). Just one teaspoon and a few minutes of wait time for a small kiddie pool does the trick. Use more for larger kiddie pools. This is a super inexpensive hack for making their pool A Little Less Toxic. The ascorbic acid costs pennies per use. I also use it to make a pool spray for before and after swimming in chlorinated pools. When you're swimming in chlorinated pools and soaking in hot tubs, it can be helpful to rinse off well before and after swimming whenever possible. The spray can help neutralize chlorine to minimize impact on your skin, lungs, or anywhere.

To make the spray: In a 16-ounce (480 ml) spray bottle, combine ½ cup (120 ml) water with ½ teaspoon of ascorbic acid or sodium ascorbate. Cover, shake, and spray down the body and hair well before and after swimming. This mix may become less effective over the days so it's best to make a new batch regularly.

Resources

At the time of this writing, these are the brands and products that I love and use in my home and would recommend to friends and others. Be mindful to continue to read ingredients labels on everything, even on the products and brands that you've come to trust and love, because they can also change. Sometimes brands get bought by bigger companies that don't have the same concern for what goes into the products. Sometimes brands change formulation and it's important to continue to just read and be informed about what you're inviting into your home.

* *A Little Less Toxic*, www.alittlelesstoxic.com: My website has all of these products and brands, with links listed, plus loads of discounts and more, so be sure to go over and visit!

* *Amazon*, https://www.amazon.com/shop/alittlelesstoxic: My Amazon shop where many of these items and more are linked.

Kitchen:

1 Aarke, https://www.aarke.com/us/: Premium Sparkling Water Maker

2 All Clad, https://www.all-clad.com/: Stainless Steel Bakeware, Cookware, & Tools

3 Almond Cow, https://almondcow.co/: Machine for making nut milk

4 AquaTru, https://aquatruwater.com/: Countertop water filtration system

5 Ball, https://www.newellbrands.com/: Mason Jars with Lids

6 Berkey, https://www.berkeyfilters.com/: Purified and fluoride-free water system

7 Bissell, https://www.bissell.com/: Steam Mop for floors

8 Bon Ami, https://www.bonami.com/: A nontoxic cleaner

9 Cannovia, https://cannovia.com/: Pure All Natural CBD Oils in Various Strengths

10 Ecover, https://www.ecover.com/: Dishwasher soap

11 Field Co., https://fieldcompany.com/: Cast-Iron Skillets

12 Hu Chocolate, https://hukitchen.com/: Chocolate Bars, Gems, Chips, and Hunks

13 Instant Pot, https://www.instanthome.com/: My most used kitchen appliance

14 Ion Biome, https://intelligenceofnature.com/: Natural Gut Support

15 Kion, https://getkion.com/: Coffee, Protein Bars, and Supplements

16 Le Creuset, https://www.lecreuset.com/: Cast-Iron Dutch Oven

17 Leefy, https://leefyorganics.com/: Powerful Real Food Tinctures That Work

18 Life Factory, https://lifefactory.com/: Glass Baby Bottles and Water Bottles

19 Mamma Mangia, https://www.mammamangia.com/: Nontoxic Cutting Boards

20 Mary Ruth's, https://www.maryruthorganics.com/: Clean Supplements for the Whole Family

21 Mountain Rose Herbs, https://mountainroseherbs.com/: Herbs, Teas, Oils

22 Organic Olivia, https://www.organicolivia.com/: Herbal Medicine Tinctures

23 Organifi, https://www.organifishop.com/: Plant Based Superfoods

24 Our Place, https://fromourplace.ca/: Always Pan

25 Pique, https://www.piquelife.com/: Quality 3rd party tested teas

26 Planet Box, https://www.planetbox.com/: Stainless Lunch Boxes for Kids

27 Primal Pastures, https://primalpastures.com/: Premium Pastured Meats

28 Pyrex, https://www.pyrexhome.com/: Glass Tupperware, Batter Bowl

29 Redmond, https://redmond.life/: Seasonings, Toothpaste, and Electrolytes

30 SaniTru, https://sanitru.com/: Multipurpose disinfectant kit

31 Shark, https://www.sharkclean.com/: Vacuum with a HEPA filter

32 Skout Organic, https://www.skoutorganic.com/: Kids and Adult Snack Bars

33 Stasher, https://www.stasherbag.com/: Food Grade Silicone Storage Bags

34 Thrive Market, https://thrivemarket.com/: Online Grocery Pantry Staples

35 Tramontina, https://www.tramontina.com/: Stainless Steel Pots & Pans

36 Vitamix, https://www.vitamix.com/us/en_us/: Efficient Blender We Use Daily

37 Wellements, https://wellements.com/: Babies and Kids Wellness Products

38 Wusthof, https://www.wusthof.com/: Knife Block Set

39 Yeti, https://www.yeti.com/: Stainless Steel Drinkware, Coolers of all Sizes

40 Yonanas, https://yonanas.com/: Turns Frozen Fruit into Yummy Dessert Fast

Laundry Room:

41 Downy, https://downy.com/en-us: Downy Ball to Release Vinegar in Rinse Cycle

42 Laundry Sorter, https://honeycando.com/: Organization & Storage for the Home

43 Molly's Suds, https://mollyssuds.com/: Concentrated Laundry Powder Soap

44 Mrs. Stewart's, https://mrsstewart.com/: Liquid Bluing for Brightening Whites

45 Puracy, https://puracy.com/: Natural Enzyme Eradicating Stain Remover

Bathroom:

46 Alaffia, https://www.alaffia.com/: Kids Bubble Bath

47 Aleavia, https://www.aleavia.com/: Microbiome Friendly Body & Hand Wash

48 BaByliss Pro, https://babylisspro.com/homepage: Hair Dryer

49 Beauty By Earth, https://beautybyearth.com/: Clean Self Tanner Tanning Lotion

50 Berkey, https://www.berkeyfilters.com/: Shower Filter without Shower Head

51 Bragg, https://www.bragg.com/: Organic Raw Apple Cider Vinegar for Hair Rinse

52 Cliganic, https://www.cliganic.com/: Certified Organic Jojoba Oil

53 Dime, https://dimebeautyco.com/: Mindful Skincare Products & Natural Perfume

54 Dr. Plotka's, https://www.mouthwatchers.com/: Mouthwatchers Toothbrushes

55 Epsoak, https://epsoak.com/: Epsom Salt for Detox Baths

56 Full Circle, https://fullcirclehome.com/: Toilet Brush with Replaceable Head

57 Innersense, https://innersensebeauty.com/: Hair Care and Styling

58 Just Ingredients, https://justingredients.us/: Real Ingredient Body Products

59 Kitsch, https://mykitsch.com/: Hair Accessories and My Favorite, Spin Pins

60 Lumineux, https://lumineuxhealth.com/: Natural Teeth Whitening

61 NakedPoppy, https://nakedpoppy.com/: Certified Clean Makeup & Skincare

62 NatraCare, https://www.natracare.com/: Organic Cotton Personal Care Products

63 Primally Pure, https://primallypure.com/: Mindful Ingredient Skin Care

64 Redmond, https://redmond.life/: Toothpaste and Bentonite Clay

65 Risewell, https://risewell.com/: Hydroxyapatite Toothpaste and Floss

66 Saalt, https://saalt.com/: Silicone Menstrual Cup

67 Sky Organics, https://skyorganics.com/: Organic Cotton Swabs & Cotton Rounds

68 Squatty Potty, https://www.squattypotty.com/: Toilet Stool

69 Wholeroll, https://www.wholeroll.com/: Organic Bamboo Toilet Paper

Bedroom:

70 3M, https://www.3m.com/: Micropore Surgical Tape for Mouth Tape

71 Avocado, https://www.avocadogreenmattress.com/: Green Mattress & Pillows

72 Coconu, https://coconu.com/: 100% Natural Lubricant

73 Lady-Comp, https://lady-comp.com/us/en/: Natural Family Planning Tracker

74 Lola, https://mylola.com/: Organic Personal Care Products, & Condoms

75 Lovability, https://lovabilityinc.com/: Clean Ingredient Condoms

76 Pact, https://wearpact.com/: Organic Towels, Linens & Clothing

77 Simply Organic Bamboo, https://simplyorganicbamboo.com/: Sheets & Bedding

78 Treat Beauty, https://www.treatbeauty.com/: Organic Good Ingredient Lip Balms

Living Room:

79 Air Doctor, https://airdoctorpro.com/: Air purifier to clean the air in the home

80 Area Rugs, https://www.rugsusa.com/: Natural Jute & Wool Area Rugs

81 Fontana, https://fontanacandlecompany.com/: MadeSafe Certified Candles

82 Grow Fragrance, https://www.growfragrance.com/: Toxin Free Air Fresheners

83 Plant Therapy, https://www.planttherapy.com/: Essential Oils & Diffusers

Outdoors:

84 Anker, https://us.anker.com/: Portable Charger Battery Pack for iPhone

85 Badger, https://www.badgerbalm.com/: Natural Mineral Sunscreen & Bug Spray

86 Bear Roots Homestead, https://www.bearrootshomestead.com/: Calendula Salve

87 Bldg Active, https://www.bldgactive.com/: Skin Repair Spray & Gel

88 Goddess Garden, http://www.goddessgarden.com/: Certified Organic Sunscreen

89 Joraform Composters, https://www.joracomposters.com/: Backyard Composters

90   Kanga Care, https://www.kangacare.com/: Sealed Wet Bag

91   Natrapel, https://natrapel.com/: Picaridin Insect Repellent

92   Sea Band, https://www.sea-band.com/: Motion Sickness Wrist Bands

93   Suds2Go, https://www.mysuds2go.com/: Portable Hand Washing System

94   Sunday, https://www.getsunday.com/: Natural Lawn Care That Works

95   Suntegrity, https://www.suntegrityskincare.com/: Skin Tinted Sunscreen

96   Wild and Pure, https://wildandpure.com/: Natural Dry Baby Wipes

Others:

* 3 Little Plums, https://3littleplums.com/: Aida is a wonderful woman and mama who educates parents on the importance of the ingredients we use and the hazards of daily exposure to toxic chemicals.

* Angi Fletcher, https://angi5.com: A dedicated warrior for true wellness as well as a wife, mama, cover model, triathlete, and depression conqueror.

* Clean Mama, https://cleanmama.com/: Offers simple supplies and routines to keep a tidy and clean home. I love her cleaning calendar.

* Dr. Courtney Kahla, https://www.drcourtneykahla.com: A holistic chiropractor and wellness advocate helping others find better health. Has an extensive directory of nervous system centered chiropractors on her site.

* Dr. Organic Mommy, https://www.drorganicmommy.com: Natasha Beck, MPH, Psy.D, Pediatric Neuropsychology is a wealth of knowledge on raising kids well and living less toxic. Creator of the activity kits we use on-the-go.

* Dr. Josh Axe, https://draxe.com/: Dr. Josh Axe, DNM, DC, CNS, has great information on all things health and nutrition and provides some great recipes as well.

* Dr. Stephen Cabral, https://stephencabral.com/: Naturopath, Ayurvedic & Functional Medicine Doctor, is the CEO and Founder of Equi.Life and has a passion for all things health and wellness with over a dozen certifications in the natural health field.

* EWG, https://www.ewg.org/: Helps provide research and data in order to make informed decisions about the products and brands you use.

* Healthy House on the Block, https://healthyhouseontheblock.com/: Gives practical solutions for creating healthy indoor spaces. Amanda also offers consultations.

* Janny Organically, https://www.jannyorganically.com/: Janny is a wife, mother, healthy living blogger, and truth seeker with tons of helpful resources and information.

* Just Ingredients, https://justingredients.us/: Karalynne is always offering a better option for conventional brands and has even gone on to create her own products with only the best ingredients.

* MadeSafe, https://www.madesafe.org/: A nonprofit organization that certifies safe products made without toxic chemicals.

* Plateful Health, https://www.platefulhealth.com/: Dr. Vivian Chen, MD, is board-certified in the UK in both internal medicine and family practice and is a brilliant doctor and incredible resource on nontoxic living and health. Her Detox Right course is the best I've ever seen and so full of helpful information you won't want to miss.

* Think Dirty, https://thinkdirtyapp.com/: Encourages ingredient conscious consumers to choose safe products by checking the rating and showing potential dangers of certain ingredients.

resources

Acknowledgments

This book is the culmination of the years (more than a decade and counting!) I've spent thinking, learning, and creating a healthier home for my family. It has mostly lived in my head or been shared in bits and pieces online with beautiful, like-minded people, and with friends and family who care to chat about such things. I would never have attempted this endeavor without the strong encouragement and incredible support of my amazing family and friends.

To Damien: You are my home. And the healthiest home of a husband I could ever dream of or imagine. Thank you for being the best husband, friend, support, and man I've ever known.

To Ezekiel and Abigail: You give even more reasons to make our home and our world a healthier place to live. Your mama loves you always. If no one else in the world ever bought a copy of this book, I'd be so happy just knowing that I had it to give to you both. You are the reason I created this.

To my mama: You have shown me that home is what you make it. You teach me to keep putting one foot in front of the other and to do so with faith and courage. I needed that for this project and for always.

To my Mommy-in-Love, Patty, Dad-in-Love, Frank, and Twin-in-Love, Lauren: Thank you for making the kids feel at home with you always, and especially during those afternoons that let me steal away to create this book.

To Amy Nelsen: I could not and would not have attempted turning these words into an actual literal freaking book without your encouragement and support. Thank you for helping me make it to the end.

To my sister, Kristen: You believe in me and I appreciate your encouragement all the time. Seeing you make your own home and life healthier brings me so much joy. You deserve it. I love you.

To my small group of wonderful friends and family who have held the long secret of this book and celebrated my journey and milestones in creating it: I cherish you. You kept me going and you bring me joy. You are God's light in the world, especially in mine. Thank you.

To the whole group at Quarto, most notably my editorial team: You gave my words, thoughts, tips, and ideas a home in this book. I never dreamed I'd be able to do something like this. Thank you for helping make this a reality.

To my wonderful photographer, Matt Bilbault: You brought my words and ideas to life and in such beautiful ways, while dealing with my antics and shenanigans. You are so gifted. Thank you.

To Justin and Jill Scarpetti: You let me take over and use your beautiful home for so many of the pictures that adorn these pages. It is a gorgeous space and it is as inviting and warm as you two are. Thank you for your friendship and generosity.

To the A Little Less Toxic community I'm so honored to be with online: It is because you have joined me in caring about and sharing about these things that I have this opportunity. I am so grateful for you. Thank you.

To every brand making less-toxic products, and especially those I've come to know on a personal level: Your work matters. Your mission is important. You're making a difference. Thank you for your tireless work and commitment to making products that help people. I am so grateful for you.

To my good and gracious God: Thank you for giving me an eternal home and a purpose and so much goodness in my temporary home.

To the one who is reading this right now: You care about making your home and this world healthier. Together, we can. Thank you for being here. Thank you for caring and for allowing my words to be a part of your process.

About *the* Author

Shawna Holman, founder of A Little Less Toxic, is a mother, a wife, and a dedicated teacher. After battling life-altering health issues, Shawna was determined to find long-lasting and healthy solutions rather than harmful quick fixes. Once she began her journey toward making radical health improvements through small life changes, she soon began taking family, friends, and then fans and followers along for the ride. By seeking out, implementing, and sharing her life transformation, Shawna motivates her audience to support their health and healing through sustainable, realistic, and mindful lifestyle changes. Since healing herself and finding solace in creating a healthy home environment, Shawna is intent on sharing her story and helping those looking to live life A Little Less Toxic. Find her online at: alittlelesstoxic.com.

Dedication

To Abigail & Ezekiel

If no copies of this are ever sold, but I have it to give to you, it has been worth every effort.

Your daddy, you both, and our God... You are the places where my heart resides.

There ain't nothin' like comin' home to you.

Index